AMERICAN VICTORIAN

Overleaf: A stair hall in a late-nineteenth-century Atchison, Kansas, home fully illustrates how imaginatively Victorians harmonized such architectural and decorative elements as wallpaper, stained glass, wainscoting, balusters, and other woodwork.

A STYLE AND SOURCE BOOK

AMERICAN VICTORIAN

BY LAWRENCE GROW AND DINA VON ZWECK

HARPER & ROW, PUBLISHERS
New York, Cambridge, Philadelphia, San Francisco, London,
Mexico City, São Paulo, Singapore, Sydney

 For information address Harper & Row, Publishers, Inc., 10 East 53rd Street, New York, N.Y. 10022.

FIRST PERENNIAL LIBRARY EDITION 1985

Jacket and text design by Frank Mahood.

Library of Congress Cataloging in Publication Data.
Grow, Lawrence
American Victorian.

Bibliography: p. 218 219
Includes index.
1. Decoration and ornament—United States—Victorian style.
2. Decoration and ornament—United States—Victorian style—Bibliography. 3. Interior decoration—United States—History—20th century. I. Von Zweck, Dina. II. Title.
NK2003.5.G76 1984 728'.0973 83-48789
ISBN 0-06-091283-9 (pbk.)

85 86 87 88 89 10 9 8 7 6 5 4 3 2 1

CONTENTS

INTRODUCTION

"The ugliest thing I ever saw," was the way a middle-aged friend recently described her mother-in-law's late-Victorian mansion. "It was so large," she lamented, "that I became exhausted just getting from the living room to the kitchen." Intrigued by these sketchy details, we asked if the house were not a stylish one for its time. "Was it ever!" exclaimed our enthusiastic hostess, but then she paused, searching for the real source of her own distaste. "In those days after World War II, Jack and I were more interested in Danish modern." How the world turns. By chance, we learned an hour later that our friend's daughter, a recent law school graduate, had just moved into such a Victorian "monstrosity" with her new husband. It had lots of room for children, we were told, and, besides, the house was already full of wonderful woodwork and other decorative touches—all things missing from the contemporary town houses they had first considered.

Welcome back, Victoriana. You've come a long way. And from all appearances, you're here to stay. Just as the Colonial-style house was reborn in the late nineteenth century, so has the Victorian house been resurrected in the late twentieth. A longing for space and good workmanship, a nostalgia for old-fashioned style and grace, a fascination with the decorative techniques and materials of a highly ornamental age—all of these qualities play a part in the Victorian revival of the 1980s. And when our interest is piqued in this decorative age, we see for the first time that old America—from Maine to Oregon—is largely Victorian, and not Colonial at all. Most of the men who went down to the sea in ships from New

Bedford and Gloucester came home to mansard-roofed cottages or Greek Revival town houses. On the California coast, enterprising miners, lumbermen, and merchants built fanciful Carpenter Gothic houses and turreted Queen Anne mansions. As more and more old neighborhoods are rescued from neglect, the delightful forms of the Victorian Age come into bright and bold relief.

The Victorian revival, however, has spread far beyond the boundaries of urban gentrification. The extraordinary designs of the craftsmen and artists of the nineteenth century are being reinterpreted in modern building and interior design. Victorian-inspired motifs and materials have brought back exuberance and warmth to the domestic scene.

American Victorian celebrates this felicitous homecoming in all of its imaginative dimensions in architecture and interior design. Not a pale imitation of English taste, the Victorian assumed a unique character in America from the late 1830s until the turn of the century. The eclectic series of revivals which define the several Victorian styles drew upon classical, medieval, Renaissance, and seventeenth- and eighteenth-century European forms and designs. While wealthy Americans continued to import some of the best decorative materials from England and the Continent, most of the ornamental trappings and trimmings were increasingly produced by craftsmen working with the jig saw and fret saw, metal templates and stamping dies, and efficient machinery that could produce miles of printed papers or embossed fabrics. Decoration for the home was, in effect, democratized in America, made available for everyone.

American Victorian illustrates how this rich legacy of the industrial revolution may be recaptured today in all of its imaginative forms. The antiques of yesterday and resourceful reproductions of classic designs are ready at hand to be used in new and inventive ways.

AMERICAN VICTORIAN

1

THE ELEMENTS OF STYLE

Opposite page: The Victorians borrowed design motifs from many different sources for architectural and interior decoration. Mantels, columns, moldings, carved and plasterwork ornaments, stained-glass panels—these and thousands of other objects were produced in countless patterns, textures, and forms. Many have been saved today as "architectural antiques" and are widely available from specialty dealers.

"But, I thought it was Victorian" was the response of one homeowner when told that the formal style of her handsome 1860s brick home was Italianate. She is right, and so are the experts who classify architectural design. There are numerous Victorian styles, and what they share in common is an explicitly romantic decorative character drawn from ancient or medieval or Renaissance sources. The history of Victorian design is formed by a progression of stylistic revivals of neoclassical, English Gothic, Italian Renaissance, and French Gothic inspiration. The essence and the genius of the Victorian is the eclectic, the imaginative blending of these historical elements.

In approaching the design and decoration of Victorian rooms today, it is extremely useful to know something of the multifaceted legacy of the nineteenth century. The character of any building is first defined by its exterior form, but unless we are dealing only with a movie set, this basic style is translated internally in hundreds of ways from the most obvious—windows and doors—to more subtle elements such as woodwork and hardware. When choosing a wallpaper or considering such ornamental elements as cornice moldings, thoughtful attention to the stylistic character of a house is important. If we are lucky, and a room has been well-preserved, the clues to successful imitation or reproduction are right before our eyes. Often, however, time has obliterated the original decoration, and intelligent guesswork is the only alternative. There are excellent models to choose from which appear throughout this book. In the end, the result will depend on our own contemporary taste and needs as filtered through the record of history.

In the Greek Manner

The neoclassical aesthetic which influenced the architecture and decorative arts of the early Federal republic gradually gave way in the 1830s and '40s to a more romantic mode. The Greek Revival style, as the name implies, owes much to the ancient world, but in the lines of the buildings and their furnishings there is a softer approach, a less rigorous adherence to form than found in the neo-Roman classicism of Jefferson and Bulfinch. In the hands of country carpenter-builders who followed the plans of Asher Benjamin, Minard Lafever, and others, the Greek Revival assumed various lines which diverged from the basic temple plan. Especially in the South, where the style survived even the Civil War, did the romantic impulse of the Victorian century find expression.

The Hermitage, Andrew Jackson's Nashville, Tennessee, home, was rebuilt in the 1830s. The line of the formal portico *(left, below)* is broken by the use of an ornamental balcony. One of the refurbished bedrooms *(left)* is decorated with reproduction early-Victorian bed hangings, draperies, wallpaper, and carpeting. Rattle and Snap, a Columbia, Tennessee, home built in 1845, fully expresses the classical antebellum style.

In the Gothic Manner

Almost parallel with the development of the Greek Revival style was the Gothic Revival. Drawing its inspiration from medieval English sources, the Gothic was considered a most proper style for churches and other public buildings. Andrew Jackson Downing popularized the style for domestic use in *The Architecture of Country Houses*, first published in the 1850s. For Downing and many others, the Gothic forms—the pointed arch, trefoil, and various types of rich tracery—were consummately picturesque. These were introduced in furniture as well as in building ornamentation. The Gothic assumed its most popular expression in the so-called Carpenter Gothic or gingerbread houses found throughout America after 1860.

Roselawn, the Bowen estate in Woodstock, Connecticut *(above, right)*, is among the most important extant Gothic Revival properties. The 1846 main house is still largely furnished with ornately-carved furniture of the period *(right)*. Roselawn is now a museum. The mid-1800s Kilduff-Ray House, Mobile, Alabama *(above, left)*, is a more modest American Gothic residence.

In the Italian Manner

By the 1850s and '60s, a fully-developed American Victorian style—the Italianate—had taken firm hold of the architectural scene. The first houses often took the form of a villa with a soaring off-center tower, loggia, and veranda. A somewhat simpler and boxier profile, which included such elements as deep-bracketed eaves, round-headed windows, and a fancy front veranda, soon became the more common sight. Both the villa and the square architectural types share certain characteristics: an asymmetrical arrangement of windows and doors, a low-pitched roof, and rounded openings. Inside the Italianate house, the fondness for curvilinear form sometimes expressed itself in furniture, as in gracefully-shaped oval parlor sets in black walnut, or in such details as French-style marble mantels and bracketed archways. The love of elegant detailing was also exhibited in the draping of windows in rich woven damasks and luxuriantly-printed cotton chintzes.

John D. Morris's fashionable brick Italian villa *(right)* was built in 1864. The Indianapolis, Indiana, mansion, now open as a museum of the Indiana Landmarks Foundation, is furnished in a dignified manner with Renaissance-Revival furniture and layers of lace and textured fabric at the windows *(above, right)*. The 1862-63 Russell House in Waterloo, Iowa, and the 1872 Victorian Mansion in Cape May, New Jersey *(opposite page: left, below and above)*, have cupolas, lovely verandas, and heavy bracketed overhanging eaves. The large first-floor windows allow for light-filled interior spaces. On the same page *(right)* are illustrated the Rococo Revival-style parlor of Camden, Port Royal, Virginia (1856-59), and the recently-demolished Hopewell House, Flemington, New Jersey (c. 1854).

In the French Manner

A tall, elongated house of symmetrical proportions, with or without a mansard roof, is often termed Second Empire in style after the reign of Napoleon III (1852-70). Built principally in the second half of the nineteenth century, a Second-Empire residence usually features a two- or three-story tower at the front, elaborate window framing, and paneled frieze boards under a bracketed cornice. An urban architectural style, the Second Empire is well-suited to buildings on narrow lots where light and space are at a premium. Inside, the rooms are high ceilinged, and the windowed bays formed by the tower fill the front rooms with daylight. In interior decoration there is little to distinguish a Second-Empire house from a contemporary Italianate dwelling, with bracketed alcoves, perhaps a French-style mantel, and fashionable suites of Renaissance-Revival furniture in the parlor and master bedroom.

The vogue for the Second-Empire style spread across America in the 1860s and '70s in expanding towns and cities. The Elliott House, Petersburg, Virginia *(above)*, was built in 1876; the San Francisco town house at right was probably built in the same decade. The master bedroom at the front of the house *(far right)* is an airy expanse admirably furnished with imposing Renaissance-Revival pieces. The cast-iron baseburner inserted in the marble mantel was used for burning coal or wood.

Summer Retreats

Summer houses, second homes for wealthy Victorians, quickly spread out in seashore villages and suburban retreats during the late 1800s. It was the Stick Style, a rambling asymmetrical concoction of large verandas, projecting towers and bays, and exaggerated structural detailing, which was often chosen for the cottage home away from home. Gervase Wheeler's *Rural Homes*, first published in 1851, popularized the idea of emphasizing the structural framing of a house. Stick-Style houses are as individualistic as their builders, borrowing scores of details from the architectural lexicon, but every cottage is designed to relate to the outdoors. As benefited a summer house, the interior was not finished in a high-style manner, but was left informal, a congenial setting for a rustic rocker, wicker table and settee, and perhaps a few plant stands, all of which could be moved outdoors on a fine day.

William Emery was a successful Kansas City merchant who returned to his Flemington, New Jersey, hometown each summer and spent the season vacationing at Roselawn *(above)*. Restored today and rid of later additions, it is a delightful confection. Lamb & Wheeler's design *(right)* for a Summit, New Jersey, cottage is more conventional than Roselawn, but equally charming. As published in an 1880s pattern book, it includes a wraparound veranda, and, above it, a broad balcony from which one could enjoy the sylvan scene.

Princely Palaces

The Renaissance Revival style is a paradigm of Victorian elegance. Closely modeled on the lines of the classic Italian urban *palazzo*, the Renaissance Revival town house embodies a restrained romanticism in its decorative detailing. Well integrated in the nearly seamless facade, usually of brick or stone, are such elements as classical window caps and belt courses which define the separate floors. Closely related to the Italianate style in form, but departing from it in composition, the Renaissance Revival style was popular in sophisticated cities from the mid-century until the early 1900s. Elegant details and objects fill the interior spaces, furnishings ranging from 1860s Renaissance Revival parlor suites to later Louis XVI-style Classical Revival pieces.

Only men of considerable wealth could afford to have homes built in the Renaissance Revival style. Counterclockwise, from upper left, are seen the J. P. Morgan, Jr., mansion, New York City (1852); the Ronald-Brennan House, Louisville, Kentucky, built in 1868 for Francis Ronald; and the interior of the George H. Corliss House, Providence, Rhode Island (c. 1875), furnished with Renaissance Revival pieces.

Turrets and Towers

For most people, Queen Anne means Victorian. But try to define this most eclectic of styles! The English monarch is of little help, for there is scant evidence in the early 1700s for such complex architectural designs. Then why not call the style Eastlake, as it still is termed today in San Francisco? Charles L. Eastlake (1836-1906), an English architect and furniture designer, comes closer to the mark. His sturdy Gothic designs, especially popular in America in the 1870s and '80s, recall the best in timbered, multigabled Queen Anne architecture. Yet, this is not enough. One must look beyond medieval details to the massing of off-center turrets and towers, the use of shingling and clapboarding, a mixture of carved and relief decoration, and, most commonly, the wraparound porch.

Picturesque Queen Anne houses are found everywhere, but are especially appreciated west of the Mississippi. Illustrated clockwise, from the upper left, are the Nunan House, Jacksonville, Oregon, built in 1891-92 from plans in a pattern book; the dining room of a Little Rock, Arkansas, house rebuilt in 1889; and the Riddell Fish House (c. 1890), Benicia, California.

In the Colonial Manner

The Victorians had their own vision of the good old days, and, by the time of the Centennial, a fondness for the figures and forms of the Colonial past was popularly expressed. What had been rejected as hopelessly old-fashioned a generation or two earlier was once again acceptable, a recurring pattern in architecture and the decorative arts. By the 1890s, symmetry had returned in facades with equally-spaced windows and doors and a flat, boxy profile. Ornamental devices such as the Palladian window, the lunette, an entry portico, and a balustraded roof line were in use again. These new homes were not, however, mere copies of Georgian Colonial dwellings. With a side summer porch and perhaps a porte-cochere, double-sash windows, and narrow clapboarding, the Colonial Revival house speaks as much of the late nineteenth century as of the eighteenth. This is even more marked in the interior, often containing a mixture of simple Colonial and ornate Victorian furniture forms.

Two turn-of-the-century homes—the McGowin-Creary House, Mobile, Alabama *(top and center)*, and a Cambridge, Massachusetts, manse *(left)*—testify to the neoclassical taste for columns and pilasters, dentil cornice moldings, and white woodwork, inside and out. Yet, mixed with such well-balanced elements are such eminently high-Victorian touches as stained-glass windows (seen on the stair landing of the McGowin-Creary House) and ornately-carved furniture. By this time, Oriental carpets rather than floral squares were used by the well-to-do for their formal rooms. More modest homes made use of braided ovals and quaint hooked rugs.

The Eclectic Spirit

A satisfactory answer to the question "What style is it?" is often difficult to come by. The Roberson Memorial *(below)*, Binghamton, New York, was built c. 1905 and is officially termed Renaissance Revival in style. A description closer to the mark would be Colonial Revival with a Second Empire roof and a neoclassical veranda. The octagonal wonder which is the Armour-Steiner House *(far right, top)* is in a category of its own, but this house, too, combines various elements, including Gothic, Second Empire, Stick Style, and Queen Anne. The 1859-60 Irvington, New York, mansion was inspired by Orson Squire Fowler's designs. Pictured below it is a truly eclectic Gothic-Queen Anne San Francisco row house (c. 1899). The builder was very much in love with Eastlake details.

Architecturally, most Victorian houses are predominantly, but not solely, of one consistent style throughout. In the waves of revival fashions that swept across North America from the 1830s until the early 1900s, stylistic lines were often blurred. Found today are many "transitional" houses which extend beyond the boundaries of one, perhaps even two formal styles; for example, an Italianate dwelling with a mansard roof and dormer windows, or a Gothic Revival cottage with an Italianate veranda and cupola. The lack of stylistic consistency certainly didn't bother the Victorians and is a source of considerable pleasure today. The builders of the last century delighted in eclecticism and sought both originality and harmony in surprising textures and forms.

2

SETTING THE SCENE

Opposite page: The tendrils of stylized crimsom nastursiums swirl in curvilinear patterns in a panel of an early Art Nouveau stained-glass window in the George Paull House, Wheeling, West Virginia.

Nowhere do the essential elements of Victorian design come more into play than in a home's architectural details—in its windows, doors, stairways, walls, and floors. In part structural, in part decorative, these common ingredients, if combined with skill and intelligence, blend together with style.

The Victorians brought together the most unlikely but pleasing combinations—wood paneling and floral wallpaper, stained glass and pottery tiles, parquet and marble flooring. Nineteenth-century Americans were both the creators and the children of the Industrial Revolution. But the artisan was still very much alive in the land. Stair builders, stained-glass artists, carpenters skilled at creating fanciful wooden ornaments, plasterers who could mold everything from brackets to complete ceilings—these and many other types of craftsmen shaped the eclectic Victorian home.

If inspiration was lacking, there were always pattern books to consult. By the mid-1800s, there were dozens of such volumes replete with floor plans, window and floor designs, patterns for moldings and gingerbread, models for staircases, and sketches of fretwork, brackets, corbels, spandrels, and scores of other woodwork forms. If ready-made supplies were lacking at the local lumberyard, manufactured components of considerable design sophistication could be ordered by mail. The nineteenth century, then, was a time of great variety in building materials. Because so much was manufactured and widely distributed, it is possible once again to recapture in the 1980s not only the spirit but the imaginative architectural expression of the Victorian Age. A new generation of dedicated artisans and manufacturers is busy at work restoring as well as reproducing the old for the new.

Opposite page: Fine hardwoods—mahogany and oak—are lavished on the main staircase of this Atchison, Kansas, residence. Wainscoting handsomely ties together the three spans. George W. Howell was a lumber merchant who selected choice grades of wood for his 1885 home, now the Muchnic Gallery. A similar but simpler design is found in a Natchitoches, Louisiana, home *(left)*. The millwork is a standard type reproduced today. The intricately carved newel post *(above)* was custom-made for a Hudson, New York, town house.

Upstairs, Downstairs

Houses grew ever larger in size during the 1800s and so, too, did the winding sets of stairs which carried one from floor to floor. Gone were the days of cramped closet tight-winders wide enough for one agile person. Staircases of monumental proportions with restful landings were built to impress and to make life easier for inhabitants and guests. As a legacy of this age of elegance, fancy newel posts still stand guard at the base of the Victorian staircase and gracefully turned or planed balusters and smoothly finished rails define the ascent from entry hall to bedroom floor.

Victorian lumber dealers stocked a variety of ready-made newel posts, balusters, and railings. If the prospective homeowner could not find exactly the right item, he could consult one of many builder's manuals and pattern books for inspiration. Because a stairway had to be extra sturdy, only quality hardwood was usually specified for these support elements. The requirement for strength, however, did not preclude a decorative treatment. Specialty millwork dealers are offering similar pieces today.

Balusters and a scrolled handrail *(right)* surround the newel post of this graceful staircase in a Mobile, Alabama, home. Alternating twisted and simply-turned balusters also delight the eye. Iron balusters *(below)* were custom-made for the monumental main staircase in the Washington, D.C. mansion of brewer Christian Heurich. Standard millwork *(below, right)* was used in the McGowin-Creary House, Mobile, Alabama.

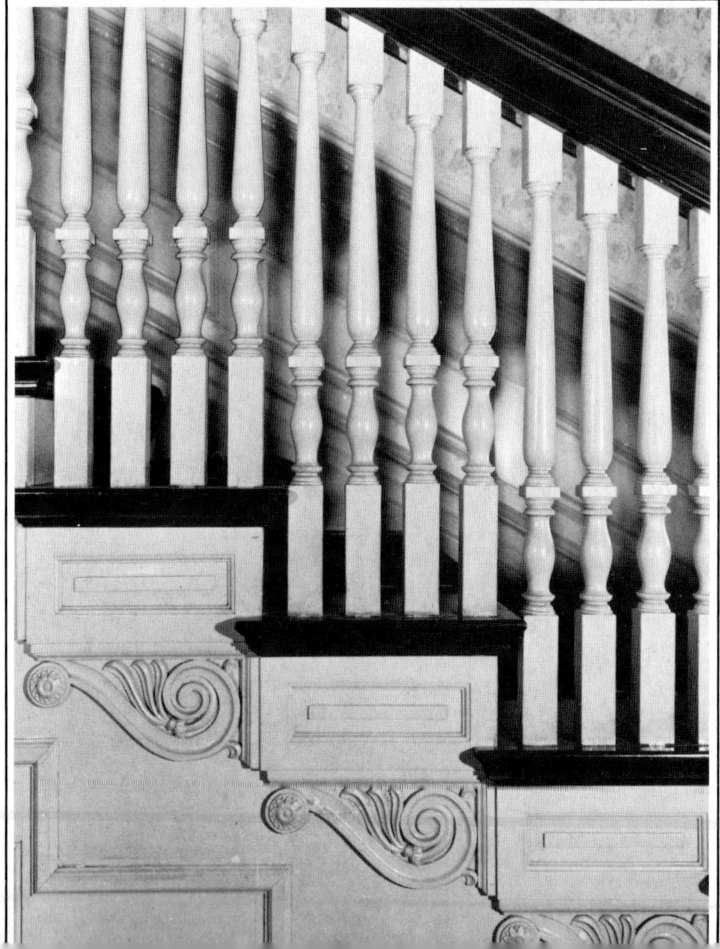

Sliding down the bannister, even such an ornate one as found in the Lockwood-Mathews mansion in Norwalk, Connecticut *(far left, bottom)*, was and is still an undeniable pleasure for children. The massive balusters would have supported even adults. Although sturdy, the fretwork balustrade of the Long-Waterman House *(far left, top)* might not have withstood as easily the trials of children. Designed in the Eastlake Queen Anne style so popular in California, the San Diego house displays such imaginative woodwork throughout. Illustrated above and to the left are designs for newel posts from William T. Comstock's 1881 pattern book, *Modern Architectural Designs and Details.*

Spiral staircases have never lost their dramatic appeal and are being built again today. During the early and mid-Victorian periods, the form was especially popular in the homes of the wealthy. In a studied formal Greek Revival interior such as that of the James F. D. Lanier Home in Madison, Indiana *(right),* the sweep of stairs defies neo-classical symmetry and, seemingly, gravity itself. The staircase, which ascends three stories through an octagonal well, terminates in a skylight.

The grand staircase in a mid-1800s Memphis, Tennessee, Italian Villa-style mansion *(opposite page, left)* gracefully winds up the curved wall of the central entrance hall. Heavy velvet cording has been looped along the inner wall in place of a rail. The outer rail returns at ground level to an elegant glass-topped swirl *(opposite page, right)*. The ball is removable, and below is a hiding place for the property's mortgage papers.

The balusters in both staircases are of a simple turned style of the type illustrated in an 1880s pattern book *(opposite page, above right)*. This type of millwork is once more being made by a number of manufacturers.

"There is nothing more ornamental about the interior of a building than a handsome flight of stairs. Above all other points let them be roomy, of easy ascent, and well lighted. . . . The effect of entering the house is pleasing if the stairs are well planned and executed. They connect the upper and the lower floors, and make the visitor understand the building and feel that he is introduced at the principal point. . . . The winding stairs, whether describing a part or the whole of a circle, can generally be made more elegant than any other kind."

Samuel Sloan
The Model Architect (1852)

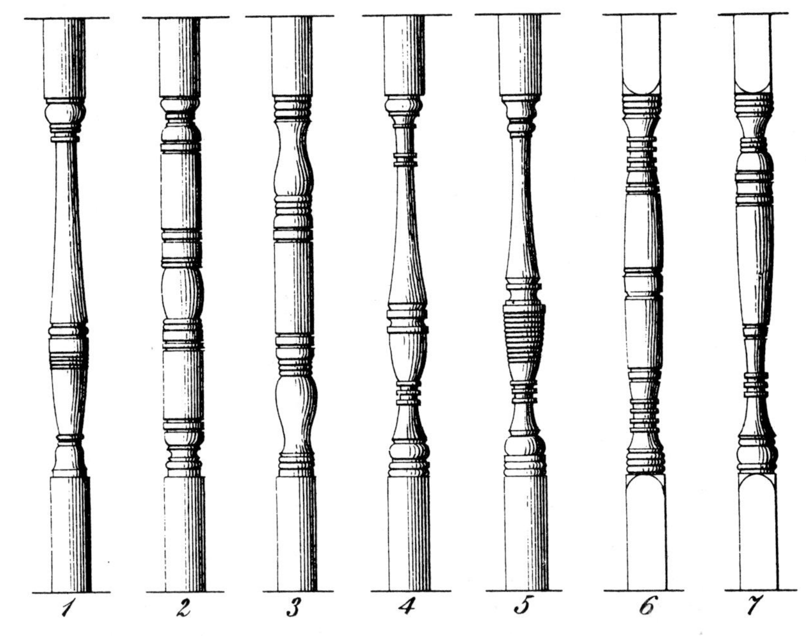

The Stained-Glass Decades

Despite their love of earlier periods of architecture and design, American Victorians waited almost half a century before realizing the decorative possibilities of stained glass, possibilities long explored in the English Gothic Revival and the later innovations of William Morris and Burne-Jones. Although imported stained glass had been used in the Gothic-Revival mansions of American millionaires, domestic production was limited to the poor work of fewer than a dozen American glassmakers. Not until 1879 was the art of stained glass accidentally reinvented. The painter John La Farge, noticing light streaming through a cheap glass toothpowder jar on his windowsill, was inspired to create a window of varying colors, textures, and opacity. Its spectacular reception brought about a burst of popular interest in the art that lasted thirty years, a period justly called "the stained-glass decades."

A stained-glass transom panel (*far left*) displays a house numeral to passers-by. Similar address panels can be custom-made to individual specifications by today's artisans. Houses on busy city streets frequently used stained-glass windows to mask out dreary urban views. The windows of New York's Villard House (*above*) and Mobile, Alabama's McGowin-Creary House (*left*) serve that purpose and filter light as well.

In the houses of the well-to-do, stained-glass panels were often incorporated into the design of ornamental woodwork and such built-in furniture as dining room sideboards. These glass panels, usually portraying objects from the world of nature, were called "picture windows," not because they bore any resemblance to today's large, single-paned windows (which they don't), but because they presented to the inhabitants of a room a vivid and beautiful "picture," framed by handsomely carved or polished wood. "Nothing in stained glass has carried further the possibilities of its art than picture windows," wrote the author of *The House and Home* in 1896. "One remembered is a picture of melons and pomegranates and grapes. Another a glass globe of gold fish hanging among morning-glories." The picture windows in the ornately paneled parlor wall of the Ballantine House in Newark, New Jersey (*far left*), represent a vineyard seen beyond colored-glass window sash.

Less elaborate than picture windows, but serving a practical purpose, are panels of delicately-tinted beveled glass (*left, top*) that allow a view of the street outside through "rose-colored glasses," as it were. Because of the current revival of interest in stained glass, much of the artistry of the craftsmen of the past has been acquired by today's workers in glass. At the left is one of thousands of glass designs adapted from the past for present-day Victorians.

Stained glass, which so suggests luxury and wealth to the modern temperament, was commonly used in houses built in the closing decades of the Victorian period. By no means was the decorative use of many-colored glass confined to the very rich. So popular was its use, in fact, that examples still abound in the surviving residences of the middle class, particularly in dining room and bathroom windows, front-door transoms and sidelights, and, especially, staircase windows.

The examples of late-nineteenth-century stained glass on this page and opposite barely hint at the decorative possibilities of the jewel-like medium, but do suggest sophisticated composition combined with subtle modulations of color and texture. The stair landing of the Hanger House in Little Rock, Arkansas (*right, top*), demonstrates how contemporary paints and modern art can actually enhance the charm of Victorian glass. At the right is the staircase of a Colonial Revival town house in Hudson, New York; its center panel features a border of opalescent glass. At the left on the facing page is the geometrically-patterned stairhall window of the Alfred Uihlein House in Milwaukee, Wisconsin. By the turn of the century, Art Nouveau was making its mark in America, and the sinewy nastursiums of a window in Wheeling, West Virginia's George Paull House (*opposite page*) are typical of the style.

"Nothing so enchants the eye as the unreal land of color that lies without and the light within as it is filtered through the beautiful medium of stained glass. These are but joys in passing. But they have power to uplift the wearied mind and to revive the sated senses.

So valuable is stained glass in a hall that, whenever possible, windows are introduced above the landings or following the turn of the stairs. These windows at different elevations are used as architectural features and in some houses are the occasions of magnificent effects in radiant color."

Mary Gay Humphreys
House Decoration and Furnishing (1896)

The Glass of the Carthusians

In matters of taste, the Victorians had legalistic minds. A new decorative style could be embraced only if it had ample historic precedents. Such was the case with etched or ground glass, a staple of Victorian style loved by anyone who has ever walked through the double-doored entryway of a nineteenth-century house. "Where stained glass would obscure daylight," wrote one arbiter of domestic taste in 1894, "there are the delicate flowing forms in which the old Carthusians in their monasteries, when forbidden to use color, used to enrich clear glass, and thus satisfy their sense of beauty." If the holy monks could decorate with ornamental glass, then so could proper Victorians.

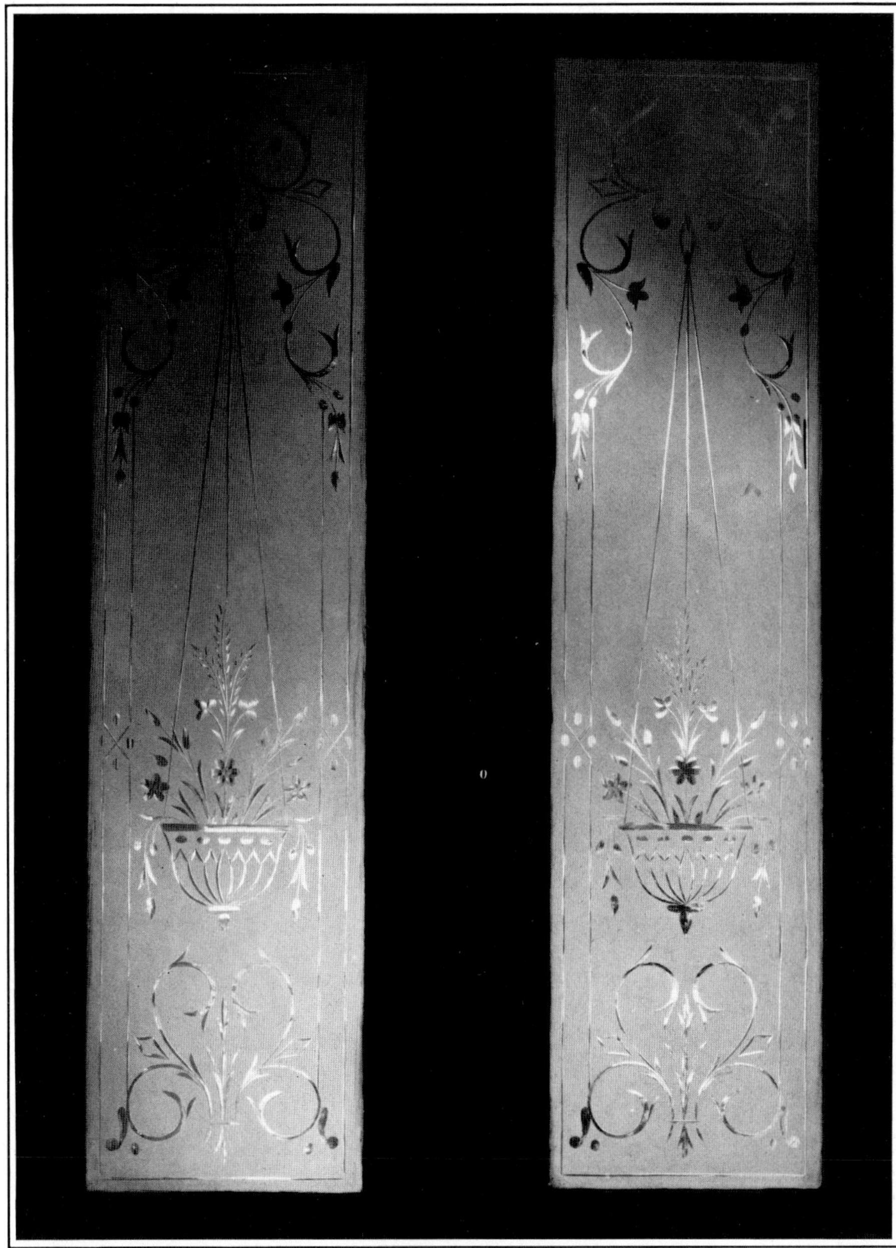

Astonishing in its variety, nineteenth-century etched glass ranges in design from motifs and emblems adapted from the Renaissance to configurations that are strikingly modern. On the page opposite *(left, top)* is a detail of a translucent window in Louisville, Kentucky's Brennan House, now the Filson Club. Below it is one of the etched beveled-glass panels in the vestibule doors of Laramie, Wyoming's Ivinson Mansion, now the Laramie Plains Museum. Similar panels, frequently used in the upper panes of windows, were the bane of hostesses whose guests objected to their relentless glare on sunny days. Also illustrated is a detail of an etched overmantel mirror in the Lockwood-Mathews House, Norwalk, Connecticut. Pictured above are the etched-glass doors of the Kilduff-Ray House, Mobile, Alabama, and the central motif of an etched-glass door in the Bidwell House, Hallowell, Maine.

Tilghman's Sand Blast Works,

NEW YORK,

81, 83 and 85 CENTRE STREET,

Manufacturers and Dealers in PLAIN and COLORED

Embossed Glass,

FOR WINDOWS, DOME LIGHTS, VESTIBULE DOORS, CARS, LANTERNS, ADVERTISING SIGNS, &c.

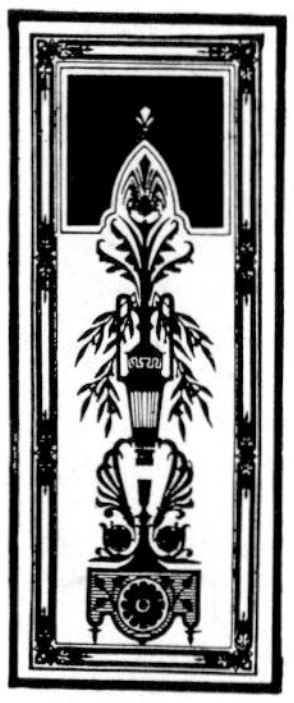

ORNAMENTED GLASS GLOBES IN GREAT VARIETY.

GLASS OBSCURED FOR THE TRADE IN ANY QUANTITY.

LANDSCAPES, PORTRAITS, FIGURES, ANIMALS,

Or any Design furnished will be Reproduced on Glass.

ESTIMATES FURNISHED.

Our Embossed Glass may be seen in the following places:

Metropolitan Life Insurance Building,
Windsor Hotel,
Chickering Hall,
Buckingham Hotel,
Staat's Zeitung Building,
Western Union Building,
Evening Post Building,
Fifth National Bank,
New York Post Office.

Oriental Bank,
Morrisania Savings Bank,
Coal and Iron Exchange Building,
Equitable Life Building,
Citizens' Bank,
Astor House,
Merchants' Exchange, Boston,
Blackstone Bank, Boston,
Baptist Church, Baltimore.

German Savings Bank, Brooklyn,
Williamsburgh Savings Bank, Brooklyn,
Savings Bank, New Orleans,
First National Bank, Denver,
Mutual Life Ins. Building, Philadelphia,
Continental Hotel, Philadelphia,
Horticultural Hall, Philadelphia,
Memorial Hall, Philadelphia,

And many other Public and Private Buildings.

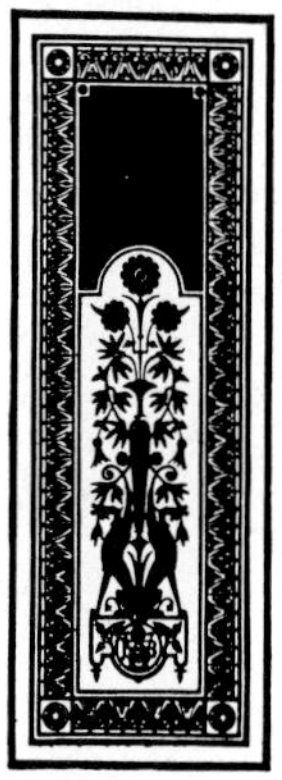

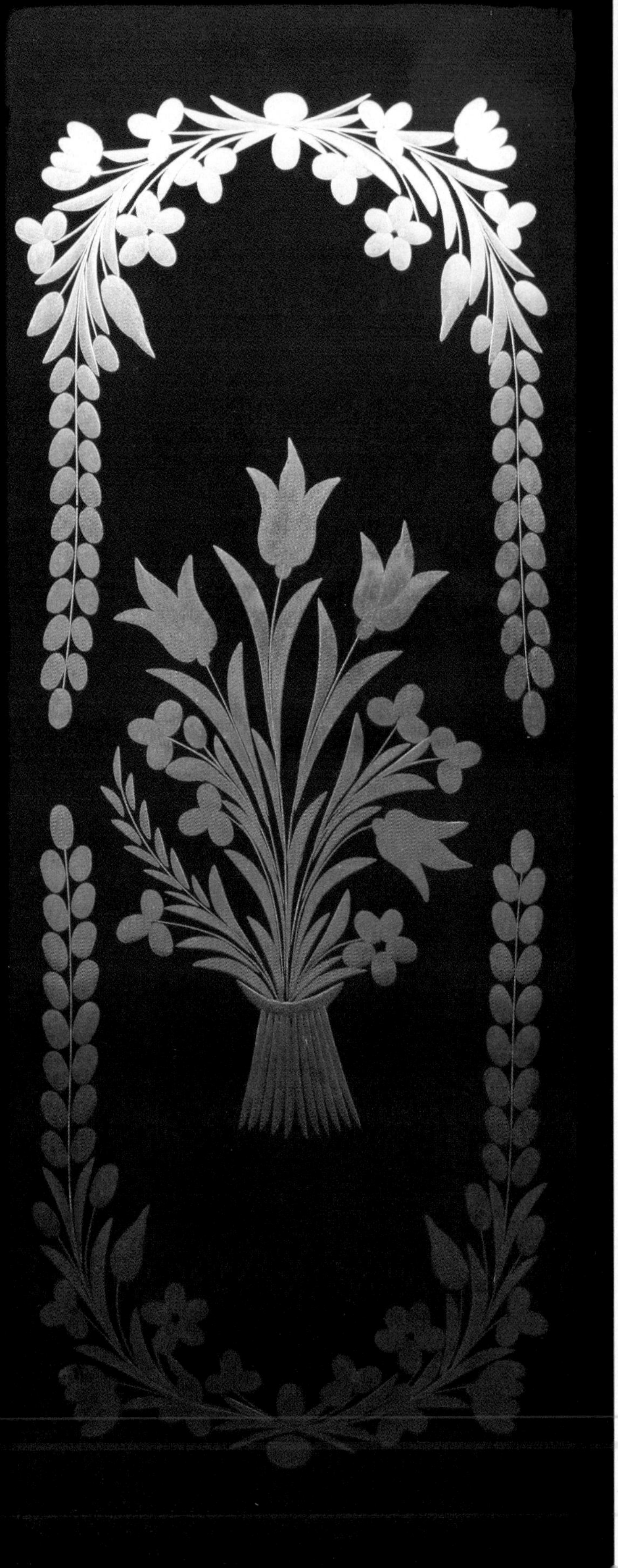

As decorated glass grew in popularity, a number of manufacturers turned their attention to meeting the demand for new motifs and designs. These ranged from the ubiquitous stag (found everywhere in Victorian objects from watchcases to toilet sets) to ornate devices copied from the Italian Renaissance. As one glass firm, Tilghman's Sand Blast Works, advertised in 1875 *(opposite page)*, its embossed glass panels contained images of "landscapes, portraits, figures, [and] animals." The company also promised that "any Design furnished [could] be Reproduced on Glass." Such is the case today, when the renewed interest in Victorian arts and crafts has revitalized the production of decorative glass along nineteenth-century lines. Many contemporary firms have, between them, virtually re-created the lexicon of Victorian etched- and ground-glass imagery. Shown on the opposite page are only two of the hundreds of design motifs available to today's consumers.

Not only clear glass was decorated. Tinted glass was also subject to the engraver's wheel, the etcher's acid. The brilliantly etched ruby glass illustrated here is from the Christian Hess House in Wheeling, West Virginia. To the left, delicately-tinted textured glass surrounds a circle of Belgian "optical glass" in a window of the Jeremiah Nunan House in Jacksonville, Oregon. The view without is thus "decoratively" magnified and distorted, a uniquely Victorian domestic delight.

In the Victorian Grain

The quality of many Victorian interiors is owed to the use of wood ornamentation—in posts and pillars, balusters and spindles, wainscoting and other forms of paneling, spandrels and brackets, and doors and windows. Because wood was plentiful and available in great variety, Americans used it more lavishly than most other peoples. While pine and cypress were utilized to the greatest extent for ornamental work because of their low cost, such hardwoods as cherry, walnut, ash, poplar, and mahogany were also ubiquitously used. These woods are most difficult to find today, but they are available in new and recycled forms. Fortunately for those re-creating the Victorian milieu, a multitude of millwork types such as interior shutters, molding, drops, and corbels are today assembled in the patterns of yesterday.

Opposite page: The second-floor landing of this Atchison, Kansas, house—now the Muchnic Gallery— is exuberantly defined and trimmed in oak. Victorian carving often takes allegorical form, as, below, in Washington, D.C.'s Christian Heurich mansion. *Right, top:* An alcove in the Tacon-Gordon House, Mobile, Alabama, is dramatically screened off from the parlor. At right are two decorative door and window designs from an 1881 pattern book.

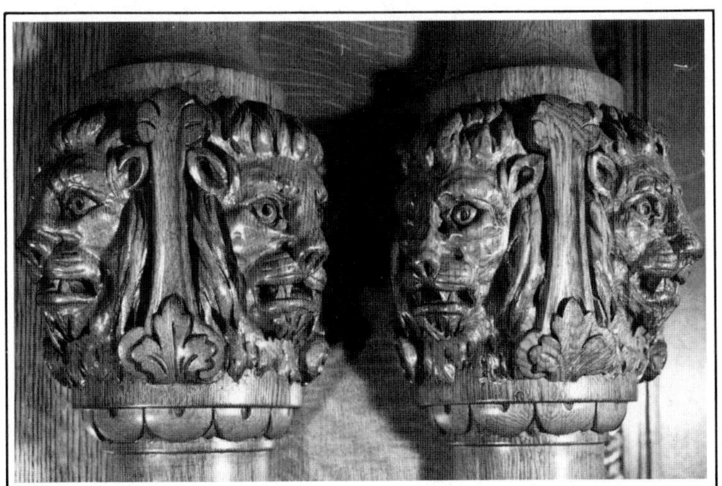

Opposite page: Oak wainscoting, mantel, window casing, and ceiling cornice produce a warm, inviting setting in the front parlor of a Colonial Revival town house in Hudson, New York. The owner's collection of art pottery and Japanese prints and the floral paper enrich the room with pleasing color. Of the many decorative woods, bird's-eye maple is among the most appealing. It is used (*above, left*) in the sliding doors of the Jeremiah Nunan House dining room. The house, located in Jacksonville, Oregon, was built completely in 1891-92 from plans in George Franklin Barber's pattern book, *The Cottage Souvenir*. The simple wainscoting, window casing, and door paneling of the McCredie House, Central Point, Oregon (*left*), stand in sharp relief to a pair of monumental carved and paneled doors from the same period (*above*).

"Gingerbread" was a term that Victorian architects detested. It conjured up, in the words of A. J. Downing, "all flimsy and meager decorations which have a pasteboard effect." However you wish to term it, the fanciful creations of Victorian carpenters are a visual delight. Although sometimes crudely and hastily fashioned by jig saw or fret saw, these touches are a welcome respite from twentieth-century modernism. They are easily and often recreated today in the woodworker's shop, and certain standard patterns can be bought through the mail, just as they once were. Most gingerbread has no structural use, but is merely ornamental. For this reason, the designs can be cut out of such lightweight softwoods as pine or birch. Although sometimes painted, gingerbread is usually only stained and varnished.

Left: A stylish staircase screen in the Samuel Tilton House, Providence, Rhode Island, lightens what could have been a gloomy corner. Similar authentic gingerbread can be supplied by firms dealing in antique woodwork.

Below are illustrated two offerings from an architectural salvage depot, one of many contemporary firms that cherish what only recently was despised.

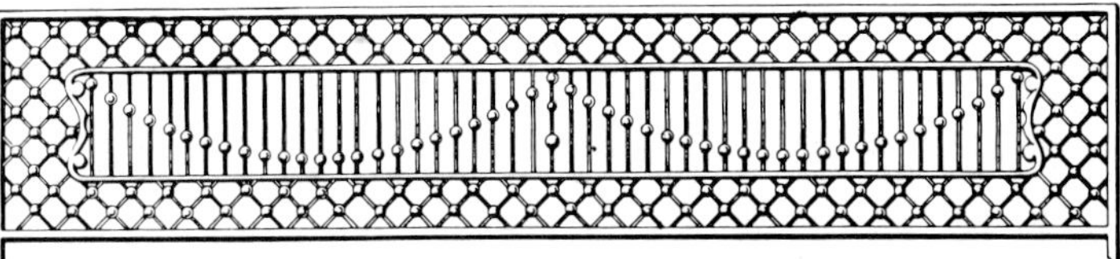

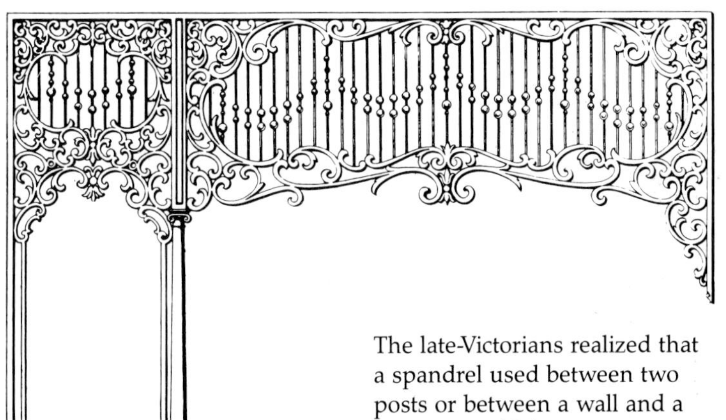

The late-Victorians realized that a spandrel used between two posts or between a wall and a support could form an attractive entryway or define the separate areas of a large room. Their gingerbread spandrels, creative fantasies in fretwork, paterae, and beading, added a touch of opulent detail to rooms already alive with exuberant colors and textures. Such Victorian gingerbread can be found today intact in surviving houses, in architectural antique shops, and in the skillful reproductions of modern Victorian millwork suppliers. Reproduction spandrels, which make imaginative use of fretwork, spindles, and latticework, surround a detail of the three-bay carved screen in the Tacon-Gordon House, seen in full on page 39.

Underfoot

Residents of modern apartments and homes, where flooring consists of little more than indoor-outdoor carpeting affixed to plywood or concrete, never cease to admire the flooring materials found in Victorian houses. They really aren't that extraordinary; in most cases flooring consists of pine planks or the equivalent of #10 oak strips. And in many homes, such common materials were fairly well hidden under a layer of carpeting until late in the century. But there *is* a floor underfoot everywhere, and today these quality wood floors, no longer buried wall-to-wall, can be polished to a handsome glow. Use of more expensive materials such as marble and encaustic tiles is usually restricted to the vestibule. Parquetry came into fashion in the 1880s, and manufactured squares (parquets) of inlaid contrasting hardwoods are found in many Victorian parlors and dining rooms.

MINTON'S

ENCAUSTIC TILES FOR FLOORS.

MINTON'S

ENCAUSTIC AND PAVING TILES,

For Vestibules, Halls, Hearths, Conservatories, etc., in Dwellings, and for

CHURCHES, BANKS, STORES, ETC.

AS LAID BY US IN THE

CAPITOL AT WASHINGTON.

GLAZED WALL TILES,

In Brilliant Colors for Grates and Fire-Places,

AND FOR INSERTION IN

WAINSCOTING, MANTELS, DOOR-FRAMES, FURNITURE, ETC.

Both kinds of Tiles are used in Panels of Brick and Stone

FOR EXTERIOR DECORATION.

Garnkirk Chimney Tops, Glazed Stone Ware Drain Pipes,

VASES for LAWNS and GARDENS,

PLUMBERS' MATERIALS,

AND FIXTURES OF EVERY DESCRIPTION, READY FOR USE.

FOR SALE BY

MILLER & COATES,

279 PEARL STREET,

New York.

JOHN W. BOUGHTON,

1118 Market Street, Philadelphia, Pa.

Manufacturer and Proprietor of

Wood Carpet, Parquet Floors,

AND WAINSCOTING.

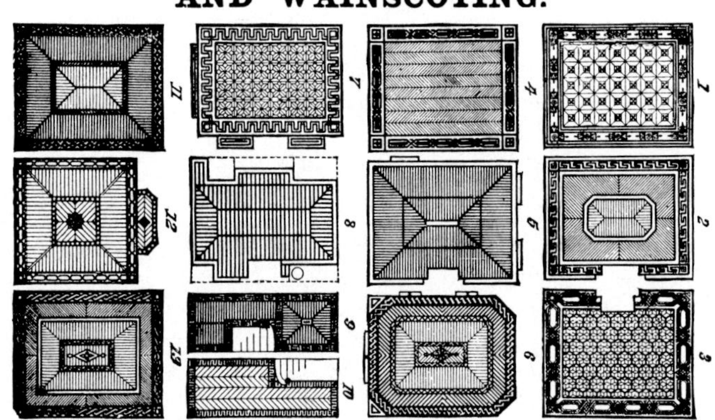

These goods have been introduced and used about eight years, and have become very popular, meeting a growing demand from wealthy people and those whose tastes are cultivated by extensive travel in foreign lands, where ornamental hard wood floors (Parquetry), are, and ever have been, universally and extensively used.

WOOD CARPET is made of strips of wood ¼ inch thick, thoroughly kiln-dried, and cemented to heavy muslin. It rolls up like an oil cloth, and is used as a substitute for CARPETS, MATTINGS, and OIL CLOTHS, in rooms of every description.

Ornamental Hard Wood Floors.

The finest Parquet Floors in Europe are successfully imitated, and at a much less expense.

PARQUET FLOORS are laid in Parlors, Libraries, Halls, Reception Rooms, &c., Turkish Carpets or Persian Rugs being used with them.

Parquet Borders

Alone are often laid around the outside of a room—filling up all the offsets—with a carpet in the center. This is a very popular style.

As a Wainscoting

These goods are used with great success, in plain stripes, or in the most elaborate designs.

Prices Of Carpet.

Offices, Stores and Kitchens, 25 cents per square foot, laid and finished.

Prices of parquet floors for parlors, libraries, vestibules, &c., from 35 cents to $1 per sq. foot.

These Goods received the Centennial Medal and Highest Honor.

Opposite page: Suppliers of specialty flooring materials often advertised their wares in building manuals. Miller & Coates touted the very English tiles of the Minton potteries which were, nonetheless, "laid by us in the Capitol at Washington." John W. Boughton spoke of his prefabricated parquetry as "wood carpet" which, in addition to being made in squares, could be supplied simply as a border. *Top, left:* Strips of alternating light and dark oak form the bedroom floor in the 1868 Brennan House, Louisville, Kentucky. A floor of hardwood such as oak or black walnut was sometimes laid over a subfloor of pine.

Special features or areas of a house such as the tower space seen at left were often floored in a unique manner. Ceramic tiles are found in the main entrance hall of Lyndhurst, Tarrytown, New York, built in 1838. The extraordinary parquet design *(above)* by the Boughton firm of Philadelphia makes lavish use of oak, walnut, and mahogany.

Affordable Luxury

Ornamental plasterwork, one of the glories of Victorian interior design, was reserved for the houses of the well-to-do, where architects could translate the wealth and position of their clients into vaulted ceilings adapted from the medieval past or lavish fantasies of classical motifs meant to simulate a Colonial past that never was. More ordinary citizens were content to limit their appreciation of expensive plasterwork to ceiling medallions for the gasoliers in their principal rooms and, occasionally, to cornices or to brackets at the base of a graceful arch. And they did so because their builders could purchase these architectural elements ready-made, just as they could order finished millwork which was frequently substituted for expensive plasterwork. The same is true today, with modern technology having made reproductions of Victorian ornament less expensive and more accessible to homeowners than the originals ever were.

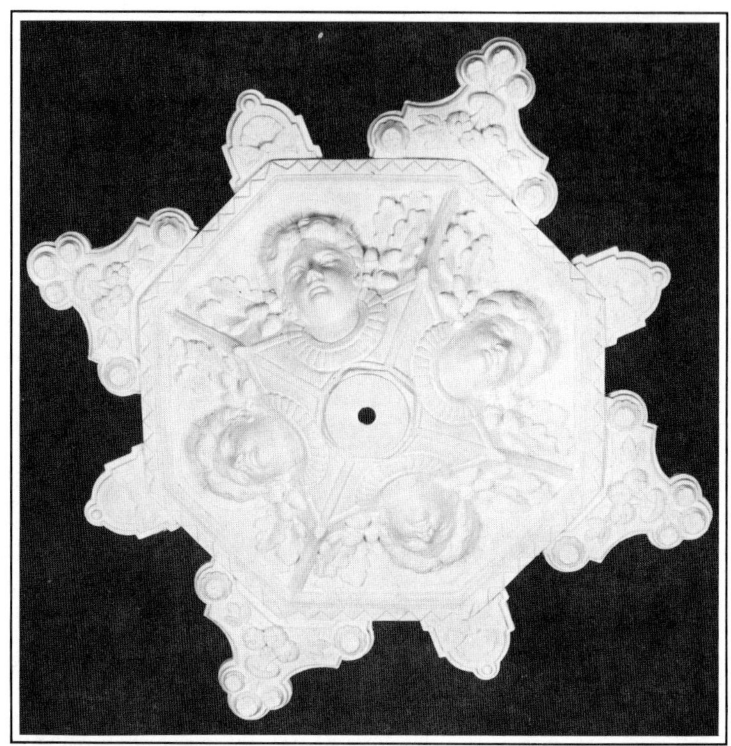

Opposite page: Medallions similar to the ornate centerpiece in the parlor of the Philip T. Berry House, Washington, D.C., can be found today in simulated versions cast in plaster from molds made from nineteenth-century originals. Shown is a modern casting of a figured medallion originally in use in a late-Victorian house in San Francisco. Pictured on the far left and far right of these pages are designs for a plaster cornice and elaborate ceiling suggestd in a pattern book of 1881. It is possible today to reproduce such complex plasterwork in fibrous composition, and even a simplified version of the cornice in the Cole Kingsley House in Rome, New York *(left, top)* and the pilasters of the Burgess-Maschmeyer House in Mobile, Alabama *(left)* could be assayed by the adventuresome.

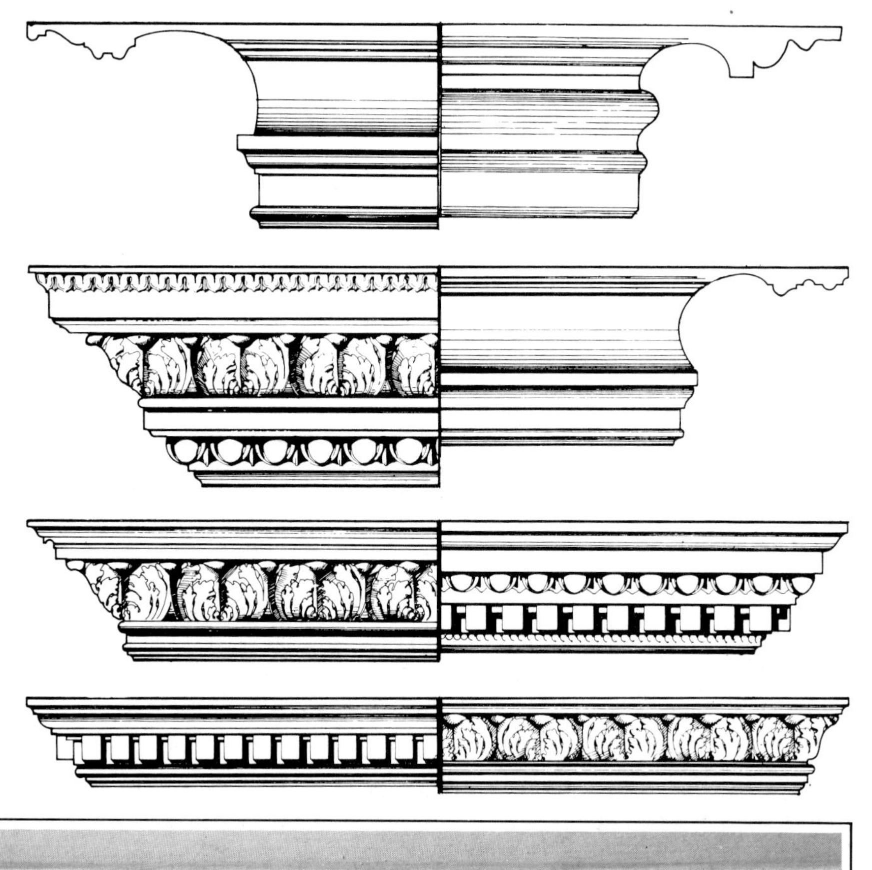

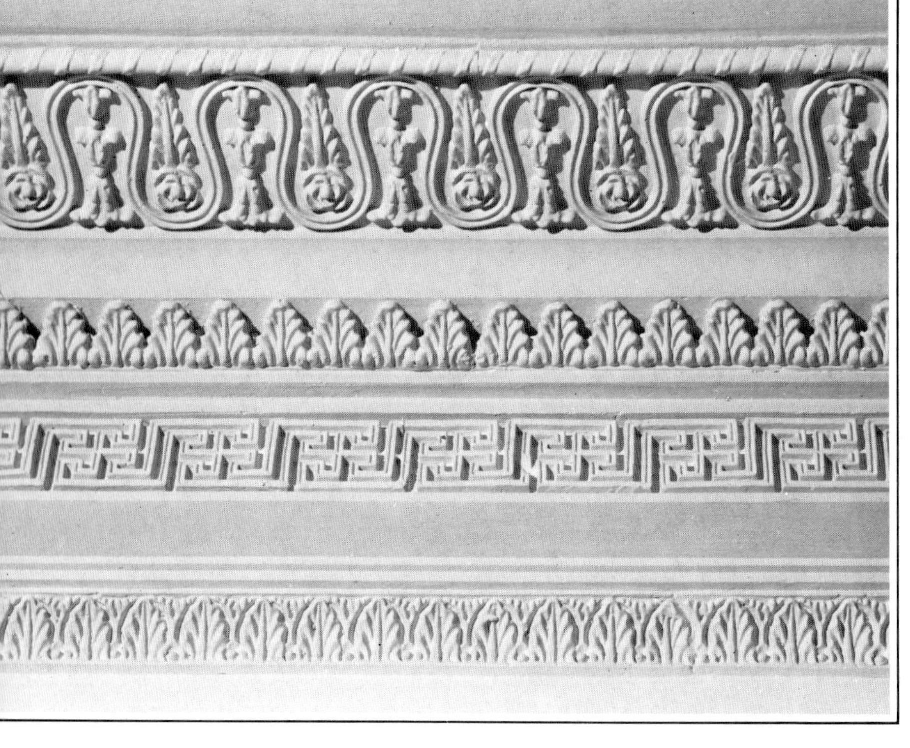

Opposite page: Designs of reproduction plaster moldings from the catalogue of a contemporary manufacturer—just eight from a selection of well over a hundred— suggest the possibility of simulating the separate elements that comprise the elaborate cornices of high-style Victorian parlors *(left, bottom)*. Plaster brackets, like those supporting the stairhall arch at Oaklands, Murfreesboro, Tennessee *(right, top)*, fill the catalogues of restoration specialists, and even gilded plaster ceiling ornaments, like those in the Lucius Tuckerman House, Washington, D.C. *(right, bottom)*, are also reproducible today.

Just how extravagantly ornamental late-Victorian plasterwork could be is evident in the drawing room of the McGowin-Creary House in Mobile, Alabama *(left)*, an interior that would have pleased the European bias of novelist and social arbiter Edith Wharton, who urged Americans "of taste" to ape the decorating schemes of their Continental cousins.

3

HARDWARE

Opposite page: The ultimate in Victorian bathing luxury, this shower, which sprays inward from all pipes, was installed in the Laramie, Wyoming, mansion of wealthy banker Edward Ivinson in 1892. Made in Chicago, and similar to showers used in Europe during the same period, the shower stall is still intact in the mansion, now the Laramie Plains Museum.

At the beginning of the nineteenth century, the term "hardware" meant chiefly mechanics' tools and builders' hardware, but it soon came to mean all small metal articles used in the construction of houses or for household purposes, tools, furnishing goods for kitchen and dining room service, tin plate, sheet iron, nails, screws, fence wire, and more. By the end of the Victorian era, it was not uncommon for a large hardware house to have in its catalogues nearly 100,000 kinds and sizes of articles, and for the giant mail-order houses of Sears, Roebuck and Montgomery Ward to offer a goodly percentage of them. Given the quantity and variety of hardware handmade and mass produced in America during these years, it's no wonder that most old houses still have original pieces intact. Guard and preserve these artifacts from the past, but, if you need to seek replacement parts, or if you have to start from scratch in furnishing your home with decorative hardware, keep in mind the small army of entrepreneurs now reproducing nineteenth-century hardware in quality and quantity almost equalling the old. Some firms can even reproduce pieces to match the old pieces original to your home.

Hardware is the stepchild of design. It is taken for granted, ignored, its very utility working against it, until it wears out and has to be replaced. Then we notice with a start, as we contemplate today's sorry little plastic knobs and metallic-painted composition screws, just how handsome Victorian hardware was. Look to the hardware and see that it matches. Like an evening gown with the wrong pair of shoes, a house may be poorly dressed without our even knowing it.

Cire Perdue Hardware

Since the great bronze masterpieces of the Renaissance, so admired by the Victorians, were produced by the ancient *cire perdue* (lost wax) process of hollow casting in metal, it is hardly surprising that manufacturers would have turned their attention to this ancient process in making decorative objects for the nineteenth-century home, hardware included. Drawing upon every possible design motif, from figurative lions' heads to geometric patterns, some of them anticipating the zigzag motifs of Art Deco by many years, hardware manufacturers decorated the surfaces of doorknobs, hinges, escutcheons, butts, doorbells, sash locks, and any other hardware that lent itself to ornamentation. In style from 1870 until well into the twentieth century, household hardware made by the *cire perdue* process is now manufactured once again, with molds made from original pieces.

WHITNEY & ROGERS,

229 Third Ave., New York,

MANUFACTURERS OF

REAL BRONZE HARDWARE,

DOOR KNOBS, BUTTS, WINDOW TRIMMINGS,

FAST AND LOOSE JOINT ORNAMENTAL BUTTS,

Ornamental Bronze Front Mortice Locks and Latches.

THESE GOODS ARE CAST IN PURE BRONZE METAL, AND ARE EQUAL IN QUALITY AND FINISH TO ANY MADE, AND ARE APPROVED BY NEW YORK ARCHITECTS.

CATALOGUES FURNISHED ON APPLICATION.

Sole Manufacturers of Empire Safety Locks, with Patent Slide Key-hole Cover and Patent Lock Staple.

In the *cire perdue* process, a model is made in plaster, coated with wax in which the details of the design are executed, and covered with a mold of perforated plaster. It is then heated until the wax melts and runs out of the holes, and molten metal is poured in the mold at the top until the metal fills the space formerly occupied by the wax. When cool, the mold is broken, the core removed, and the metal polished. The chief advantage of this process is what made it so attractive to Victorian manufacturers—*cire perdue* requires far less metal than other casting techniques.

Although bronze hardware made by the lost-wax process is not only handsome, but sturdy, the same process was used in the manufacture of inferior goods from cheaper metals. Builders warned about the folly of such low-cost hardware. "As a rule," wrote E. C. Hussey in *Home Building* (1875), "the most expensive character of locks, knobs, and other builders' hardware, is that which is sold for the smallest sums; especially does this rule apply to door furnishings . . . as there is nothing which gives house-keepers so much annoyance as to have the locks and fastenings getting out of order."

Shown on the opposite page is an 1891 advertisement for *cire perdue* hardware. To the left are examples of similar hardware from the 1895 Montgomery Ward catalogue, which cleverly hawked "Geneva bronze" (iron made to look like bronze) as well as the real thing.

Plain and Fancy

The notion of the Victorian era as an age of excess is just not so. In matters of utility, American machine-made objects—sleek farm tools, stripped-down carriages, simple hardware—were admired throughout the world. "The redundant must be pared down, the superfluous dropped, the necessary itself reduced to its simplest expression," wrote the Yankee sculptor Horatio Greenough in 1852. In Victorian America, plain and fancy coexisted.

Simple functional objects and the same objects highly decorated were available to Victorian consumers. The objects at the right, both plain and fancy, appeared in the 1897 Sears, Roebuck catalogue. Porcelain hardware *(below)* was made throughout the second half of the nineteenth century and could be purchased in solid colors or in mottled patterns.

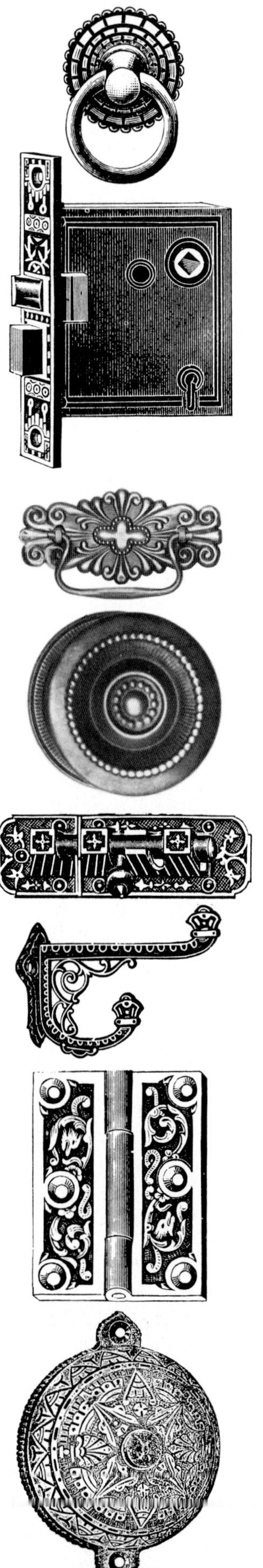

Kitchen Call Boxes

Every period has its servant problem. Ours is that we don't have any; the Victorians' was that they found it difficult to summon theirs. During the nineteenth century the old-fashioned bellpull that brought the downstairs upstairs was superseded in the houses of the well-to-do by speaking tubes, and later, in the age of primitive electricity, by annunciators with their little falling shutters in glass windows that summoned servant to master electrically.

While no longer practical objects of kitchen hardware, annunciators are delightful accessories in Victorian homes. Servants' signal boxes, if not already in place in an old house, can be found occasionally in antique shops. Clock dealers, especially, are a good source since several manufacturers made combination clock/annunciators *(right.)*

Bathroom Hardware

After years of being unfairly maligned as hideously ugly and out of date, the Victorian bathroom has staged something of a comeback, and a small industry has sprung up to service the needs of people enamored of porcelain tubs on claw feet, wooden-tanked pull-chain toilets, and shiny nickel accessories. While few people would willingly sacrifice the conveniences of a modern kitchen to the backbreaking appliances of the nineteenth century, the delight of Victorian plumbing is an entirely different story. With the exception of dispensable whirlpool baths and California hot tubs, there are no features of the modern bath that did not have their more handsome antecedents in the nineteenth century. All elements of the Victorian bath are available today as antiques or as skillful reproductions. Not for nothing was a recent biography of Thomas Crapper, the Victorian inventor of the toilet, called *Flushed with Pride.*

Like most bathrooms of its day, the wainscoted bathroom of the James Whitcomb Riley House *(left)* contains a china basin set in marble and a metal-lined wood-encased bathtub. The nickel-plated tumbler holders are not much different from those illustrated in the 1897 Sears, Roebuck catalogue *(opposite page).* Almost every bath accessory sold by the great mail-order firm ninety years ago is sold by specialty dealers today, making a fully-equipped Victorian bath within easy reach of anyone who wants one. Also on the opposite page are antique water closets, one with a crystal pull chain and cherrywood tank and seat *(above)* and the other, ornately patterned.

BATHROOM AND LAVATORY FURNISHINGS

AT REDUCED PRICES.

We have secured an exceptionally fine line of bathroom fixtures, and at prices we believe your saving will average nearly 50 per cent. They are made of brass, heavily nickel plated, and with ordinary care will last a lifetime. Do not compare these prices with the shoddy bathroom fixtures sold by other concerns.

BATHROOM TRIMMING OUTFIT - - - - $1.98

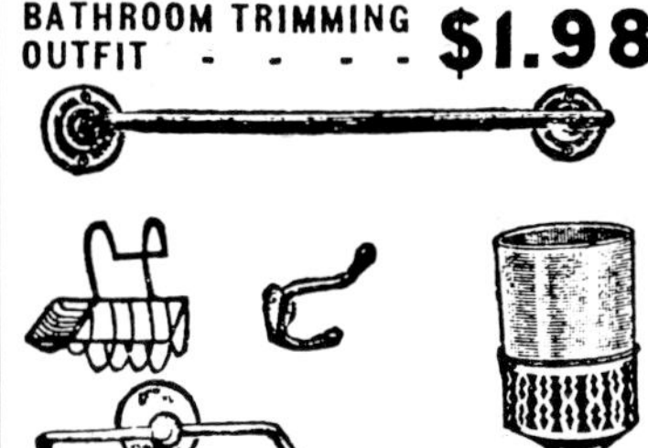

No. 42K1109 For the convenience of our customers we have gotten up this set, which consists of the most necessary bathroom trimmings, namely, an 18-inch towel bar, combination sponge and soap holder, towel hook, paper holder and combination toothbrush and tumbler holder. Each of the above articles is made of brass, highly nickel plated, and we know that anyone of our customers purchasing one of these outfits will be highly pleased with it. The tumbler or toilet paper is not included in price quoted below. Weight, about 3¼ pounds.
Price $1.98

Single Robe Hooks.

No. 42K1110 Brass Nickel Plated Single Robe Hooks. Come complete with screws. Weight, 1½ ounces.
Price, per dozen, $1.05; each 9c

Soap Dish.

No. 42K1134 Brass Soap Dish. Heavily nickel plated, with heavy brass ball feet. Size, 3x4½ inches. A very handsome soap dish. Weight, 10 ounces.
Price 24c

Soap Cups.

No. 42K1140 Soap Cups for the rim of the bath, solid brass, nickel plated, finely finished. Hanging rods can be adjusted so as to fit any tub. Size, 6x3½ inches. Weight, 10 ounces.
Price reduced to 46c

Combination Sponge and Soap Holder.

No. 42K1151 Heavy Brass Nickel Plated Soap and Sponge Holder, 9x10 inches. Weight, 1 pound. Price.....$1.12

Tooth Brush and Tumbler Holder Combined.

No. 42K1160 Brass Nickel Plated Tooth Brush and Tumbler Holder. Height, 4½ inches. Weight, 7 ounces. Price reduced to 44c

Combination Tumbler and Soap Holder.

No. 42K1165 Combination Tumbler and Soap Holder. Made of brass, heavily nickel plated. Size, 5½x8 inches. Weight, 12 ounces. Price.......83c

Towel Rack.

Nickel Plated Towel Rack. Made of heavy brass, heavily nickel plated. Strong and durable; finely finished bar is ½ inch in diameter; projects 2½ inches from wall. Average wt., 8 oz.
No. 42K1180 Length, 15 in. Price..27c
No. 42K1181 Length, 18 in. Price..30c
No. 42K1182 Length, 24 in. Price..33c

Extra Heavy Towel Rack.

No. 42K1187 Extra Heavy Towel Rack. Made of brass, nickel plated, with cast brass posts. Diameter of bar, ½ inch; width from wall, 3 inches. Weight, about 8 ounces.
Length, 15 inches. Price reduced to.....47c
Length, 18 inches. Price reduced to.....48c
Length, 24 inches. Price reduced to.....52c

No. 42K1222 Rubber Covered Brackets, heavily nickel plated, oak board, 6x18 inches, well finished. Furnished with either steel or brass rods. Weig't 3½ pounds.

Bath Tub Seat.

Price, steel rods, nickel plated 47c
Price, brass rods, nickel plated 72c

Toilet Paper Holders.

No. 42K1227 Stamped Brass Nickel Plated Paper Holder. Size, 4x5½ inches. Weight, 4 ounces.
Price..............12c

24c

No. 42K1228 All metal Parts made of cast brass, heavily nickel plated, the roller or wood part is highly enameled. Weight, 6 ounces.
Price.............24c

No. 42K1233 This is one of the neatest and best Toilet Paper Holders on the market. It is made of brass, heavily nickel plated, and at the price we ask for it is a bargain. It must be seen to be appreciated. For people wanting a high grade holder we feel confident this one will give satisfaction. Weight, 9 ounces. Price.........................62c

SHOWER BATH YOKE, WITH 6 FEET OF HOSE $1.12

No. 42K1247 A lady can use it without wetting her head. Each limb can be showered separately, placing the arm or leg through the yoke. There is no splashing of walls or floor, as the sprays or jets of water are directed inwardly and flow over all parts of the body. This yoke is made of brass, highly nickel plated, and will last a lifetime. Weight, 12 ounces.
Price......$1.12

$1.12

No. 42K1248 Same as above, except it is highly nickel plated and is furnished with a patent tip which can be attached to any faucet.
Price.....$1.28

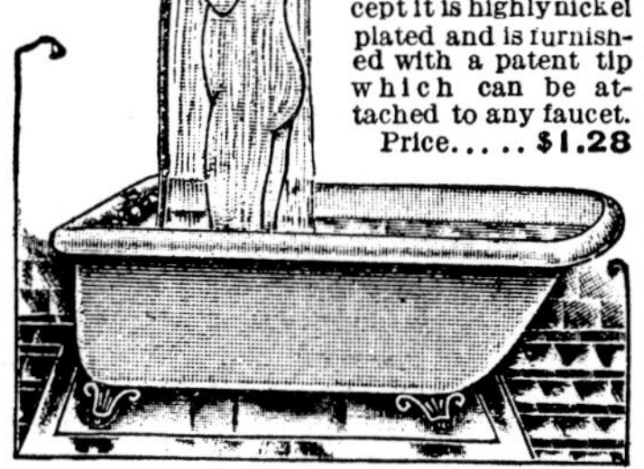

Compression Basin Cocks.

At Reduced Prices.

No. 42K1267 Compression Basin Cocks, T handle. Made of brass. Heavily nickel plated. Weight, 1 pound.
Price reduced to......60c

80c

Nickel Plated Basin Cocks.

No. 42K1272 Low Down Nickel Plated Basin Cocks, with cross handles and china tops, indexed hot and cold. Quality, A1. Weight, 1 lb. Price..80c

4

WALLCOVERINGS

Opposite page: The late Victorians delighted in Oriental art and design. This floral wallpaper pattern of the late 1870s anticipates the vogue for Japanese design motifs of a decade later.

Colorful wallcoverings in floral, geometric, and architectural designs are a hallmark of the Victorian period. It was in the 1840s, the first complete decade of the British Queen's long reign, that mass-produced papers of exceptional artistry were made commercially available. The popularity of wallpaper for home decorating—in the parlor, front hall, dining room, and master bedroom—increased in America with the passing years. Thousands of patterns and many types of printed materials were offered in a variety of finishes.

As the Victorians knew well, a sprightly or stately wallpaper pattern can establish an interesting stylistic mood in any area of the house. One, two, and even three papers can be used in various combinations to define space effectively, to make it worthy of attention. And, as homeowners of every era have discovered, papering is a convenient way to hide the unlovely, the cracked plaster ceiling or, simply, the boring expanse of blank wall. Paint may cover over the nicks and scratches, but it is a poor substitute for the decorative dimension supplied by a paper.

The visual delights of Victorian papers have not been left in the dusty past. They may be found as close as the neighborhood paint and paper store in countless reproductions, adaptations, and ageless standard patterns which no amount of twentieth-century commerical sterility can extinguish. While a fortune can be spent easily on custom-made historical papers, most of what is available and appropriate to accent the Victorian setting is hardly more expensive than the same amount of oil-base paint.

From Single to Multiple Patterns

The most simply decorated Victorian rooms are usually found in houses built in the 1840s and '50s. Although inexpensive wallpaper printed on high-speed roller presses had begun to replace block-printed papers, fashion lagged behind economy except in the most sophisticated urban centers. The spare, restrained approach to decorating usually resulted in the use of only one paper in a room. When two or more were chosen, the additions were likely to be narrow borders or solid-colored papers suitable for use in the area between the chair rail and the floor. Borders, used to prevent soiling, were also cut from the principal paper and run around doors and windows in a direction different from the overall pattern.

Opposite page: A simple c. 1860 cottage parlor is enlivened with the use of three papers from Schumacher's Victorian Collection, "Queen's Aviary" being the principal pattern. It is outlined by a rope border; a solid and sober design, "Queen's Filagree," is used below the chair rail. *Above:* One dominant flocked paper from Scalamandré lavishly decorates the high-style dining room of Fountain Elms, Utica, New York. An Italian Villa-style mansion built in 1850, it is now the home of the Munson-Williams-Proctor Institute.

Fanciful floral and geometric patterns remained popular throughout the 1800s, although more naturalistic designs gained the decorator's favor in the 1880s and '90s. Not as frequently used in Victorian interiors as one might think are such supposed all-purpose favorites as the cabbage rose design and red flocked papers. The nineteenth-century housewife had much more to choose from than these two standards, as does today's decorator. The floral design used in the master bedroom of the 1872 James Whitcomb Riley House in Indianapolis, Indiana *(below, left)*, is effectively combined with a stenciled frieze pattern of garlands and geometric elements in gold. The background color of the paper is a rich brown shade which blends in well with the picture rail and the darker walnut bedroom furniture.

Garlands and abstract designs also appear in the "Fountain Elms" paper *(above, left)* used in the master bedroom of the house for which it is named. The original paper used in the 1850 mansion has been reproduced by Scalamandré and is available by special order.

Fabric was rarely used in American homes as wallcovering as it was in the great houses of Great Britain and the Continent. American printers, however, specialized in the production of papers which simulated the line and texture of expensive textiles, one example of which, a pattern from the 1870s, is illustrated on the opposite page.

There is ample precedent for using contrasting papers in the same or adjoining rooms—even if the effect might seem dizzying. Actually, the combination can be pleasing. Many homes from the 1800s were built with only a minimum of interior ornamentation, and, as is even more the case today, a paper can be used as a striking substitute for such detail—on ceilings in place of cornice moldings, and even to simulate paneling.

Below: Four different wall and ceiling papers can be seen in this 1890s photograph of three areas of the J. A. St. John House, Boston. *Opposite page:* Reproduction papers ranging in pattern from the early- to the late-Victorian period are widely available today. Shown clockwise from upper right are five Scalamandré patterns: Rosson Walls, c. 1900; Peterson House, 1880-1900; Strobel Frieze, 1830-40; Pimpernel by William Morris, 1876; and Thomas Wolfe Memorial, 1880-1900.

Opposite page: Just how imaginatively two or more papers can be used in the same room is illustrated in a parlor of the Tacon-Gordon House. This late nineteenth-century residence in Mobile, Alabama, has more than ample space for effectively applying a ceiling paper, a cornice paper, and, below the picture molding, a panel or "fill" paper. As the detail shows, each paper is clearly delineated. Ceiling papers are rarely of a darker shade than the side wall patterns, but with a room of this height, the progression of light to dark from floor to ceiling seems natural and uncontrived.

Right: Oriental designs were especially popular in the 1880s and '90s and took several different forms. The most expensive wall coverings were embossed leather or paper designs imported directly from Japan. There were also highly stylized "Anglo-Japanese" papers, usually imported from England and featuring naturalistic motifs in an asymmetrical arrangement. The most widely used designs were simply based on Japanese themes taken from needlework or pottery. One such imitative wallpaper pattern, from the early 1880s, is illustrated here.

Borders and Friezes

Decorative borders and friezes multiplied in variety during the Victorian era. The first designs were neo-classical in style; by the mid-1880s, floral and geometric motifs predominated, and these remained popular until the 1900s. Narrow borders can be used effectively around doors and windows as well as above a chair rail or picture molding.

Wide frieze papers are delightful substitutes for highly ornamental cornice moldings.

Opposite page: Today's reproduction border and frieze papers are appropriate for various types of Victorian interiors. Clockwise from upper right are several period papers reproduced by Scalamandré: Nathaniel Russell House Frieze, early Victorian; Rose Swag Border, 1890-1900, from the Central City, Colorado Collection; a French Classical Frieze and the Charleston Frieze, both early Victorian; Toombs House Border, 1850-70; and Rosson House Frieze, c. 1900.

Above: Only a solid or very lightly patterned ceiling or frieze paper could possibly be used along with the repetitive Japanese design which covers the walls of a bedroom in the Jeremiah Nunan House, Jacksonville, Oregon. The paper is, in effect, a series of borders.

Two different approaches to using wallpaper are illustrated in Little Rock's Reichardt House *(opposite page)* and in an Alexandria, Virginia, town house *(left)*. The front parlor of the Reichardt House is a purist's delight. Little has changed since the room was papered in the 1890s. In contrast, the town house bedroom was recently redecorated in an eclectic manner with reproduction papers from several Victorian decades. None of these patterns produced by Schumacher were intended to coordinate, yet they work well together. The wallpaper is "Sarah's Delight" and is matched with "Kerchief Border." "Queen's Filagree," a minute pattern, is used for the ceiling.

Which approach is "correct"? Both. The only rule is that patterns should be chosen with an eye to color and harmony and a concern for a rough approximation of historicity.

Since papering is no easy task, almost as much attention must be paid to the work involved as to the choice of patterns. In any such job, five important points are useful to keep in mind:

1. Always buy more paper than you estimate you will need.
2. Test a paper for colorfastness and staining before you buy it by dampening a sample with water.
3. Do not fall for the convenience of pre-pasted papers which are difficult to position correctly.
4. Make sure that all the rolls of a given pattern are from the same print run.
5. Check that all surfaces to be papered are properly prepared.

Creating Texture and Form

In place of fancy plasterwork, rich wood paneling, or a luxurious fabric, Victorians often turned to specially embossed papers, a composition material known as Lincrusta-Walton, and stamped or tooled metal for walls. These were useful for such decorative accents as cornices, wainscoting, and friezes. Although the manufacture of Lincrusta-Walton ceased some years ago, imitations of this substance are available today; the other materials are also reproduced, sometimes from original molds.

Opposite page: Strips of Lincrustra-Walton still embellish the dining-room walls of a Hudson, New York, town house. (For a view of this room, see page 129.) Among the modern substitutes for the material are Anaglypta and Supaglypta, both of which are offered by restoration suppliers. *Clockwise from upper right:* Embossed papers used in the front hall of the Bowen House, Woodstock, Connecticut; an antique embossed paper, "Acanthus Frieze," used between 1890 and 1915, and available today from San Francisco Victoriana; a sampling of stamped metal patterns which are suitable for ceilings, wainscoting, and friezes; a hand-tooled copper frieze panel from the entry hall of a California house.

5

LIGHTING

Opposite page: Created to accommodate the incandescent bulb, these lamps by the Tiffany Studio blend turn-of-the-century technology with hand-wrought craftsmanship. Patented in 1899, the lamps boast graceful bronze supports and shades of opalescent glass mosaics.

The nineteenth century produced a plethora of lighting devices unlike any seen before. The development of new fuels, a resulting flood of patented devices in which to use them, and the birth of modern mass-production methods combined to bring about a profusion of lamps and other lighting artifacts now prized by collectors and used again in period rooms. By the end of the 1800s, the centrally-served systems of gas and electricity rendered all previous lighting technology obsolete. It was a century of unprecedented progress.

But it was also, to modern eyes at least, a period of unprecedented beauty, a period in which gasoliers and parlor lamps and girandoles and newel-post lights were made of every available material that could catch the dancing flames of gas and kerosene and wax to illuminate the nineteenth-century room. Glass and brass and ormolu, wood and iron and porcelain—these were just some of the materials that went into the making of Victorian lighting fixtures.

True antique classics of the pre-electric age are not difficult to find today, particularly gasoliers and kerosene lamps. But they do command high prices. Fortunately, a healthy and imaginative reproduction industry has developed in recent years, producing handsome and fitting lighting fixtures for the Victorian setting. Particularly in the reproduction of decorative chimneys, globes, and etched-glass shades, most often made from original nineteenth-century molds, these firms have made it possible to dispel contemporary gloom with Victorian light.

Unchanged in appearance since it was redecorated for a coming-out party in 1896, Reichardt House in Little Rock, Arkansas, exhibits all of the qualities of design that have brought about a renewed appreciation of Victorian decor in modern times. Simple but sturdy woodwork defines the separate areas of the dining room and reinforces the nineteenth-century notion of the home as a man's castle, a solid refuge from the cares and worries of the world outside. The love of color and the inventive possiblities of combining unlike elements to create an effect of brilliant harmony are both evident in the use of six different papers, five of them visible in this photograph, to cover walls and ceiling. The decorative effect—the suggestion that this basically simple room has all the architectural features of a grand *palazzo,* from handsome frieze to crown cornice and paneled ceiling—stems from the skillful selection of seemingly disparate papers. The room's centerpiece, of course, is the six-lamp gilt-bronze gasolier, now electrified, but still suggesting through its polished metallic sufaces and etched-glass shades how gaslight would have illuminated this beautiful room.

Pictured above and at the far right are two gasoliers representing styles roughly thirty years apart. The brass fixture at the right, with grape leaves decorating the curvature of the arms, dates from c. 1855; its shades were added after 1876, when wide-based shades were first introduced to reduce flickering. The other gasolier, in zinc and brass, was made in the 1880s.

The Gaslight Era

The gradual acceptance of gaslight as the most progressive mode of nineteenth-century illumination made possible the *general* lighting of domestic interiors. Before the Victorian period, candleholders and early oil lamps provided concentrated light for small areas of a room, but overhead lighting was a rarity limited to public buildings and the houses of the very rich. An almost immediate result of the widespread use of hanging gasoliers was a freer arrangement of household furniture. Chairs could be moved from the sides of a room to surround what became the standard feature of almost every Victorian parlor—the center table. With antique fixtures still available, if expensive, and with reproductions made by an increasing number of contemporary firms, no Victorian parlor or dining room can afford to be without an electrified gasolier.

Rural houses could be illuminated by gas through the installation of automatic gas machines *(left)* that worked on the principle of impregnating air with the vapor of gasoline. Such machines consisted of a basement air pump operated by a weight which forced a current of air through a gasoline-filled generator in an underground vault outside.

"The advantage of gas-light is manifest. It is much cheaper, compared with the light it affords, than any other. It saves a deal of time and labor, which would otherwise be expended in filling and trimming lamps, cleaning candlesticks, and snuffing candles. Its light is agreeable and, if properly managed, gives no smoke."

Advertisement for Archer & Warner (1850)

When the parlor of the James Whitcomb Riley House was photographed in 1900, the house and its furnishings were already three decades old. The brass and crystal gasolier, original to the room, has round glass globes typical of gasolier shades before wide-based shades were introduced in the Centennial year. The fixture also features pull-chains for adjusting the level of the flame, a lighting innovation added about the time the photograph was taken. Unlike other kinds of nineteenth-century lighting, gas fixtures—with one exception—were permanently affixed to wall or ceiling. The exception was the portable gas lamp, seen on the Riley parlor table and in the advertisement on the right.

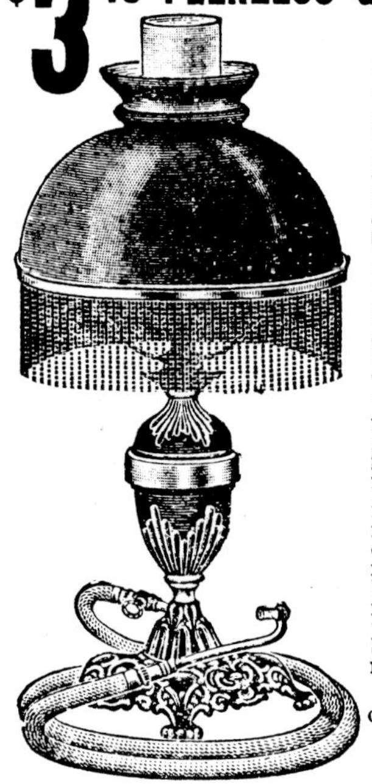

A high grade reading lamp for parlor and library, furnished complete, green shade and tubing. The lamp is all ready to use when you receive it. All that is necessary to do is to remove the gas tip from the fixture and slip in the gooseneck. Then turn on the gas and light it. **The price we ask includes all the parts, including burner,** which is of best quality, being made of polished brass; high grade **cap mantle,** opaque **chimney globe** with air holes, **green shade** (green outside, white inside), fitted with a heavy **green bead fringe** to match, and six feet of the best quality of **mohair tubing** fitted with **brass gooseneck. A high grade lamp.** We are able to offer our customers a high grade reading lamp, and for those desiring a high grade lamp we believe this outfit will give perfect satisfaction. The stand is made of metal, finished in a rich black color. The metal is highly ornamented and trimmed in polished brass. A lamp of this quality and finish together with all the fittings we give has never been sold before for less than $5.00 and more often at $7.50.

No. 3K2191 Peerless Lamp, complete and ready to light. Price.............. **$3.48**

As a general rule, gas fixtures of the early Victorian period, when gaslight was far more rare and expensive than it became at the end of the century, are much more ornate and elaborately designed than later gasoliers. Pictured here are three fixtures of the 1850s: a five-arm brass gasolier trimmed with ormolu grape vines and made by the Philadelphia firm of Archer & Warner; a decorative gasolier topped by a discreetly-draped cupid, charming to our eyes but ridiculed a generation later in the 1890s; and a portable gas lamp complete with connecting tube.

Newel-Post Lights

There is no debating the dramatic effect of a gas standard atop a newel post that lights the way before a sweeping central staircase. Debatable, however, is the widespread belief that only the very rich Victorian could afford them. On the contrary, wise homeowners then as now realized that ingenuity runs a close second to a heavy purse. It was not difficult at all for the man of average means to afford a modest newel-post light. Taking their cue from watch and clock makers, Victorians were intrigued with the economy of interchangeable parts. Millwork suppliers were no exception and sold the makings of a newel post in mix-and-match patterns. Any number of bases could be fitted with any number of screw-on finials. Substitute a lamp-fitted bronze statue (dozens were sold by lighting manufacturers) for a finial and, *voilà*, instant luxury, instant drama!

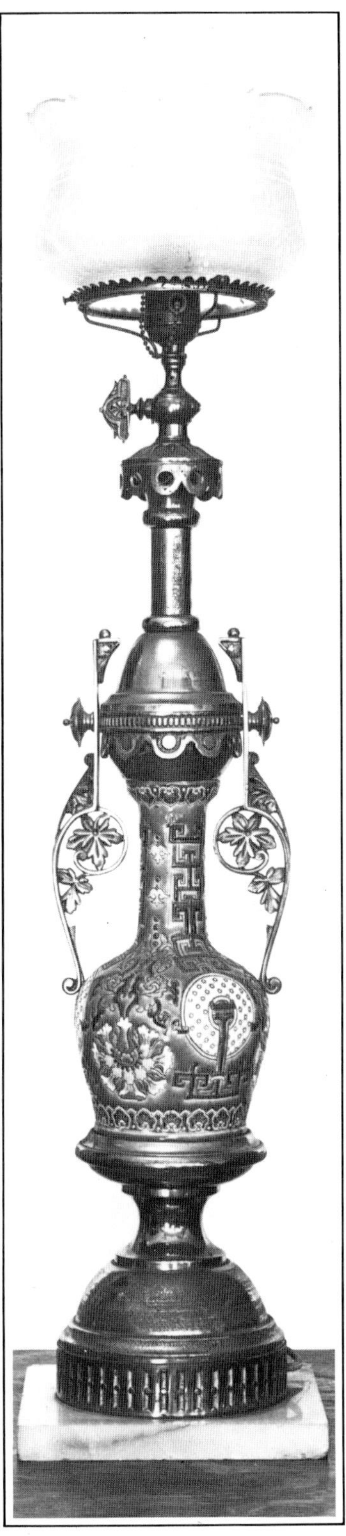

Gas standards mounted on newel posts were far more common in the nineteenth century than one might expect. Conditioned as we are by Hollywood's evocation of the age of gaslight, we associate the illuminated newel post with the mansions of the Robber Barons and their social set. Although the well-to-do most certainly installed some sumptuously ornamented examples in their villas and estates, the middle classes could choose from hundreds of more modest styles listed in the catalogues of such lighting manufacturers as Philadelphia's Cornelius & Sons. Illustrated here are four gas standards that range in style from the lavish to the relatively simple. The Christian Heurich Mansion *(opposite page, left)*, built in Washington, D.C., in 1892 to meet the exacting standards of a millionaire brewer, boasts a newel-post fixture that would not be out of place in any public building of the period. The Morse-Libby House *(opposite page, right)*, built in Portland, Maine, between 1859 and 1863 for a hotel magnate and decorated lavishly by the New York artist Giuseppe Guidicini, features a pair of enormous bronze statues as staircase standards. More typical of the statuary used by the ordinary Victorian is the newel-post light in the Robert Machek House, Milwaukee, Wisconsin *(far left)*. The house was built in 1894, a time when bronze figures were adorning everything from mantelpieces to clocks. To the right is a gas standard decorated with polychromed ceramic inserts in the Anglo-Japanese style and very popular in the 1880s.

Sconces and Brackets

Far more common than centrally-fixed chandeliers, although used in conjunction with them in the houses of the affluent, were wall fixtures that throughout the nineteenth century were made for every mode of lighting. Sconces for candles, usually with shiny metal or mirrored reflectors to intensify dim candlelight, were standard fixtures of the previous century and continued to be made throughout the Victorian period, even though they were gradually superseded by brackets holding oil lamps. Although oil and gas fixtures virtually coexisted in time, their use depended in part upon the economic circumstances of their owners. After 1860 kerosene oil was cheap and plentiful, while gas was available only to the urban upper classes and to those rural homeowners who could afford private gas plants in their houses. Those who could afford them used gas brackets particularly by bedroom washstands and dining room sideboards.

Wall fixtures were commonly used above bedroom washstands and almost always in conjunction with a mirror for reflected brilliance. The gas sconces above the double washstand in the Morse-Libby House *(right, top)* have elbows that enable them to swing in front of the mirror for added illumination. Such fixtures, when they could not be conveniently electrified, were sometimes replaced in the early twentieth century by a single lightbulb and glass shade on a dangling electric cord. Stationary sconces and swinging brackets for kerosene lamps were common favorites in rural households. The examples to the right and on the facing page, all with reflectors, were featured by Sears, Roebuck in 1897 and are still made.

Sconces and brackets were made throughout the nineteenth century for every mode of illumination—from candles to electricity. Illustrated here *(clockwise from upper left)* are a candle holder in the dining room of Lyndhurst, the Gothic-Revival mansion in Tarrytown, New York; a gaslight fixture in the shape of a morning glory in the parlor of the Ronald-Brennan House, Louisville, Kentucky; three early electric wall fixtures; and a kerosene bracket.

The Ubiquity of Kerosene

When petroleum, from which kerosene is derived, was discovered in Pennsylvania in 1859, it not only created a new wave of American millionaires, but it also provided an endless source of oil for the nation's lamps. Kerosene burns brightly, is relatively clean, and, because of its abundance, is unusually cheap. As a continuous stream of improvements perfected the efficiency of kerosene burners, kerosene lamps became the primary mode of lighting in America during the second half of the nineteenth century. No matter the other means of lighting used in the home, kerosene lamps were always present.

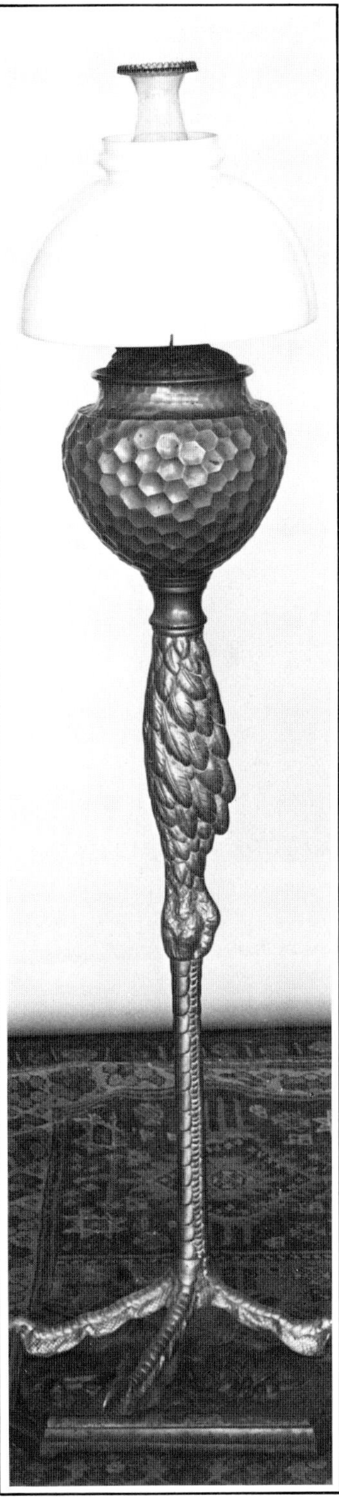

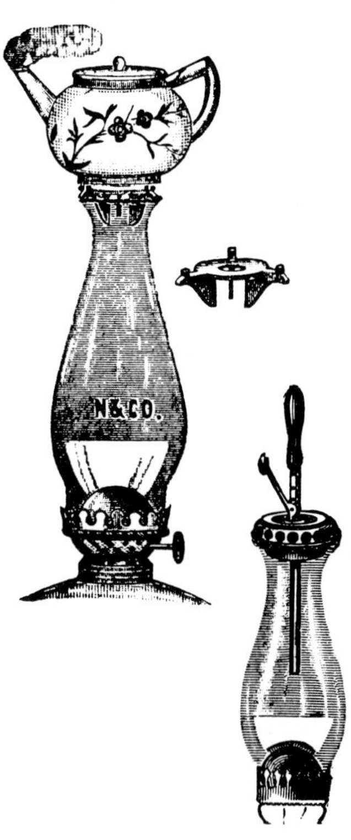

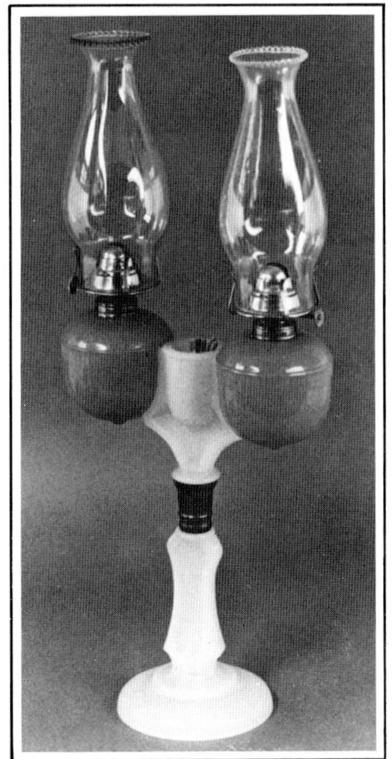

The early Victorian parlor of the Morris-Butler House *(opposite page)*, Indianapolis, Indiana, includes among its furnishings several oil and kerosene lamps, including an astral lamp on the pianoforte, a kerosene floor lamp, and an ornate kerosene lamp on the center table. Illustrated on this page *(clockwise from upper left)* are a turn-of-the-century painted-vase parlor lamp, often called a "Gone-with-the-Wind" lamp because of its anachronistic use in the famous 1939 movie; an 1880s floor lamp with an unusual bird's-leg base; another painted-vase parlor lamp; two ingenious devices for heating tea water or curling irons on lamp chimneys; a "bride's" or "marriage" oil lamp, c. 1870; and a fancy parlor lamp with beaded fringe.

The student lamp, cantilevered from its stem so that light could be placed directly over a book or work surface, was introduced by Carl A. Kleeman of Erfurt, Prussia, in 1863, but was not widely used in the United States until the 1870s. Thereafter it became one of the most popular lighting devices ever used.

Student lamps proved immensely popular not only because they burned with a bright, steady light, but because of the excellence of their design. *Clockwise from upper left:* A student lamp adorns the desk in the library of Lyndhurst, Tarrytown, New York; an advertisement for a late-model student lamp in the 1908 Sears, Roebuck catalogue; the 1897 Sears model; a display of student lamps illustrates the variety of shapes and sizes taken by the form.

Clockwise from upper left: A kerosene lamp hangs from the plank and beam ceiling of the Van Spankeren House in Pella, Iowa; of the three hanging lamps advertised in the Sears catalogue for 1897, the two on the left (like that in the Van Spankeren House) are called "library lamps," while the one on the right is designed for the hallway; two 1897 kerosene chandeliers; and a chandelier in the French style.

Although portable oil lamps preceded the introduction of gaslight, hanging oil and kerosene lamps first developed as fashionable imitations of the centrally-fixed gasolier. Once gas chandeliers became popular, hanging kerosene lamps became the vogue where gas was inaccessible or unaffordable.

A mirror in the Ronald-Brennan House parlor *(left),* Louisville, Kentucky, reflects both a turn-of-the-century table lamp by the Tiffany Studio and a brass gasolier with ornate art-glass shades. The Tiffany shade, a mosaic of opalescent glass, is patterned with naturalistic chrysanthemums. The gasolier shades reflect the decorative tastes of the 1880s and later, when shades, and even the lamp chimneys within, sported etched or painted designs and crimped and tinted edges.

Opposite page: The renewed interest in Victoriana has brought about a minor business boom in the lighting hardware industry. Glass shades, many made from original molds, are now available in a profusion of designs that rival the contents of nineteenth-century lighting catalogues. Shown here are only a few of the hundreds of reproduction shades on the market today. The handsome 1880s gasolier at the far left is fitted with replacement shades delicately etched in a paisley pattern. The single shades illustrated *(clockwise from upper right)* include three gasolier shades that are snowflake etched, floral etched with amber edges, and satin frosted; a shade in a graceful upward-turned leaf pattern; a shade in which frosted and clear glass are combined; a shade in the shape of a cluster of grapes and available in a variety of colors, from amber to cobalt blue; and a tall vase-like shade in fluted crystal-clear glass.

The Play of Light and Shade

What makes a lighting fixture pleasing to the eye is not merely the outline of its shape or the materials from which it is made, but the play of light against the surface of its decorated shades. Victorian glassmakers were masters of the art of designing and decorating chimneys, globes, and shades as fixtures of every lighting mode were introduced and improved upon. Their heirs, today's reproduction experts, offer as wide a variety as was manufactured in the past, their wares often made from original molds.

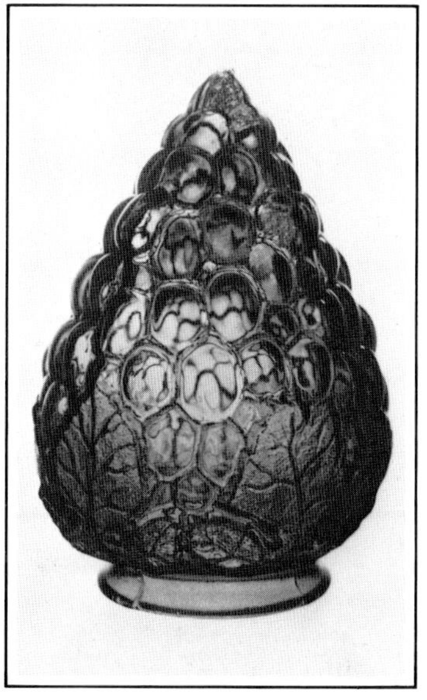

Mr. Edison's Invention

In 1879, after months of fruitless experiments, Thomas Alva Edison succeeded in making an incandescent lamp in which a loop of carbonized cotton thread glowed in a vacuum for over forty hours. Thus began a lighting revolution that led eventually to the wiring of the world. The benefits of electric light were immediately recognized—illumination at the turn of a knob, with no fuel fonts to fill, no wicks to clean, no smoke to soil draperies and walls. But one innovation of Mr. Edison's invention is almost lost on us today. For the first time in history, the source of light could be directed downward as well as up. As a result, many early electric fixtures, taking full advantage of this dramatic novelty, looked like nothing that had come before them.

In transitional lighting fixtures, gas burners always face ceilingwards while incandescent bulbs point downwards. Seen here *(clockwise from right)* are an 1895 advertisement; an 1895 photograph of a Washington, D.C., dining room equipped with a transitional chandelier and matching sideboard lamps; and two antique combination gas and electric lighting fixtures.

The chandelier in a bedroom of the James Whitcomb Riley House, Indianapolis, Indiana *(upper left)*, was originally all gas-lighted. The electrical elements were added in the early 1900s. Dripping with its original crystal beading and prisms, the transitional gas and electric fixture at the upper right has coordinated shades decorated with etched wreaths.

The triumph of electricity is visible in the Boston parlor of J. A. St. John, photographed in the late 1890s. The thirteen-branch electric chandelier is totally unlike contemporary gas or oil ceiling fixtures. Its designer has incorporated the shape of the incandescent bulb into the fixture's overall design. The c. 1905 ceiling fan/light fixture *(below)* is completely unlike today's flimsy reproductions.

The Glow of Candlelight

Although it was eclipsed in the nineteenth century by a succession of more modern modes of illumination, the ancient and humble candle never passed completely out of use. People of means, mindful of good taste and grumbling at the graceless conveniences of modern life, were growing nostalgic for simpler times. "It was a great deprivation when we were obliged to give up candles for gas," complained Clarence Cook in *The House Beautiful* (1881). "Nothing could be prettier than the effect of a room prepared for an evening party, decorated with flowers and lighted with wax candles. Candlelight is the only artificial light by which beauty shows all its beauty—it even makes the plain less plain." Large numbers of his contemporaries agreed and turned to the use of some of the most beautiful candleholders ever made.

Above: The soft glow of candlelight would have been present everywhere in the monumental dining room of Lyndhurst, one of the grandest Gothic Revival houses in America—in silver candlesticks, enormous chandeliers, and shaded sconces.

Candleholders of every shape and size and of every available material were used throughout the Victorian era. The examples illustrated on this page can only approximate the inventive variations played upon the candlelight theme. Pictured above is a c. 1840 design for a Gothic-Revival chandelier. Shown clockwise from upper left are a candelabra made in 1840 to mark the New York debut of the dancer Fanny Elssler; a pair of pressed-glass candlesticks in the form known as "petticoat dolphins," made in Pittsburgh in the 1860s; a pair of sterling candlesticks made by the Gorham Mfg. Co. at the turn of the century; a pair of pressed-glass candlesticks made by the Boston and Sandwich Glass Co. in the 1840s; and a combination gas and candle sconce.

6

DECORATIVE PAINTING

Opposite page: From the stained-glass panels in the double doors to the painted plaster medallion on the ornamented ceiling, the hallway of a San Francisco town house vibrates with light and color and is saved from the gloom that has overtaken similar entryways through the years. The decorative painting is by itinerant artist Larry Boyce.

Since the romantic Victorians doted on periods of history earlier than their own, it is only natural that they would have rediscovered, reinterpreted, and revitalized many of the ancient arts, decorative painting among them. The Italian Renaissance, together with the Gothic Middle Ages the primary source of Victorian inspiration, had itself rediscovered the art of painting walls and ceilings perfected by the Greeks and Romans it so venerated. This discovery prompted a revival of the art in the courts and churches of Europe, a revival that lasted well into the eighteenth century, when changes in technology and the beginnings of industrialism enabled a wealthy middle class to ape the fineries of court life in their own estates and villas. By the nineteenth century, exuberant Victorian craftsmen once again rediscovered decorative painting. Using stencils, stucco, and machine-made papers, they created dazzling interiors that rivaled in color and ornament the bright, polychromed exteriors of their spacious houses. Although the very rich alone could afford the luxury of frescoed walls and ceilings, the popularity of stenciled decoration, frequently combined with wallpaper and painted moldings, was fostered by the editors of women's magazines and other household manuals who abhored the "blank chilliness" of stark kalsomine and whitewash. Even farm wives, whose avoidance of the fancy was considered a social virtue, were urged to learn the techniques of stenciling and to tint their ceilings and walls. The pages that follow should move us moderns to contemplate with shame our own unpainted surfaces and to discover once again a long-neglected art.

A Century of Color

Vibrant color was the hallmark of the nineteenth century and perhaps its greatest gift to those of us chilled by modern glass and steel. In matters of design, the Victorian era was in many ways more democratic than our own. The good taste of the rich was expected to become the good taste of all. As one observer wrote in 1896, "Both color and form may be translated from material to material, from brocade to cotton, from dollars to cents, and lose nothing in their real value. A color scheme worked out in costly frescoes may be as artistically valuable elsewhere in stencils or in kalsomine."

Victorian decorative painting is endlessly inventive and ranges from the delicate tinting of plaster elements already in place to the imitation of those elements exclusively through the medium of paint. In the parlor of the 1872 Benjamin H. Epperson House in Jefferson, Texas *(opposite page, left),* is a frescoed center medallion from which is suspended a splendid gasolier; a frescoed band, simulating an architectural cornice, runs around the edges of the ceiling. Epperson, a wealthy man, could well have afforded plaster decoration, yet he selected stylish imitations in paint.

The Governor Henry Lippitt House, built during the Civil War in Providence, Rhode Island, is an excellent example of a Renaissance Revival residence with fine intact interior decoration. Its elaborate interiors feature the use of many woods, marbles, stenciled walls and ceilings, and chandeliers. The stenciled ceiling *(above, left),* based on Renaissance patterns, is punctuated by architectural rosettes.

The exquisite decoration of San Francisco Plantation in Reserve, Louisiana, was painted in the 1850s when the property was named St. Frusquin. It has been restored to its mid-nineteenth-century magnificence after years of being buried under what one Victorian observer once called "pigsty whitewash." The decorated ceiling of one parlor *(opposite page, right)* and the unusual painted French doors *(left)* of the other are superb examples of the stenciler's art.

"From the nature of ceilings, the manner of finishing them is susceptible of a wider range than the side wall affords, however ornamental the latter may be. The reason of this is apparent when we consider that the ceiling is the only portion of an apartment which is not covered up or obscured by furniture or ornaments, and that the eye rests upon it undisturbed by surrounding objects. . . . Until lately, good taste had been so little developed that it was agreed for dwelling-houses in general that a plain white ceiling was the best. . . . But we are at last beginning to learn that the blank white ceiling may be relieved from its cold chilliness by tinted paints, ornamental papers, fresco painting. . . ."

Almon C. Varney
Our Homes and Their Adornments (1883)

The library of the 1871 James Whitcomb Riley House, Indianapolis, Indiana *(above, right)*, is ornamented with handsome stenciling. The gray walls are capped by a stenciled border of a garland design in greens, with pink and white flowers. The ceiling has a stenciled geometric design, with a blue background and rose, gold, gray, and black elements. The cornice, which separates border and ceiling, is painted in hues of gray. The lavish architectural features of the front hall of the George H. Corliss House in Providence, Rhode Island *(right)*, are actually *trompe l'oeil* paintings.

Now a museum known as Victoria Mansion, the Morse-Libby House in Portland, Maine, was built between 1859 and 1863 as a summer villa for Ruggles Sylvester Morse, a New Orleans hotel owner. Designed by New Haven architect Henry Austin, the mansion was one of America's first houses built in the towered Italian Villa style, and is certainly one of its finest.

The music room, a corner of which is shown on the left as it appeared before restoration, is typical of the luxurious interiors of the spacious house, each room of which is lavishly decorated in a period style thought appropriate to its use. A sumptuous blend of fine architectural detail and colorful frescoes, the music room recalls the age of Louis XVI in its painted grandeur. In decorating it, artist Giuseppe Guidicini undoubtedly drew on eighteenth-century sources for his inspiration. A generation earlier, in the age of Jackson, the appearance of winged *putti* on the walls of a Yankee house would have been considered downright un-American.

The rich fruit-and-flower-patterned plaster cornice of the music room is real, unlike the painted *trompe l'oeil* cornices of some rooms in the house. The work of Guidicini and his eleven assistants is so expert that it is difficult to differentiate architectural art from architectural artifice.

Painted decoration can achieve dramatic effect when employed in combination with disparate elements of Victorian design. The parlor of Montauk, an 1874 Italianate house in Clermont, Iowa *(left)*, plays a stenciled border of vines against starkly plain walls and ceiling, an effect that is at once subtle and vivid. Becky Witsell's restoration of the library of Little Rock's Reichardt House *(above)* to its appearance in 1896 combines a painted chair rail, a silk-screen painted reproduction of the original fan-palm paper border, a painted cornice, and a papered ceiling.

"Stenciling," wrote Mary Gay Humphreys in *House Decoration and Furnishing* (1894), has vivacity, subtlety, and those elements of surprise that ward off monotony from our surroundings, and which can never be found in machine-printed paper." She might have been writing about the ceilings of the stairwell landings at Chateau-sur-Mer *(below)*, the 1852 Newport, Rhode Island, mansion, remodeled in the 1870s by Richard Morris Hunt. Here stenciled ivy vines sprout incongruously above the balustrades.

Frescoed ceilings, like those in the Morse-Libby House *(above)*, were the envy of middle-class Americans, who, by the 1880s, were able to decorate their ceilings with patterned papers that imitated more costly fresco.

Back in 1881, one E. H. Leland, advising housewives on the decoration of their rooms, brought up the subject of stenciled painting. "If a lady has a little talent and a little leisure for the work," he wrote, "she may devote an hour or two each day to the coloring of borders and ceilings at the tops of tinted walls. A leafy pattern in grape, ivy, or other trailing vines, with a bright bud or berry peering out here and there, could be outlined with the aid of pasteboard patterns, and the colors neatly laid on with small brushes. A few feet of this stenciling finished each day would be no great tax on her time, and when all was completed she would have a charming artistic relief for the plain, softly-tinted walls." "Such decoration," he warned, "should not be attempted unless one has a genuine 'knack' for it."

Self-help manuals have always made things sound easier than they really are. Although he certainly has a "genuine 'knack' " for stenciling, Larry Boyce admits that painted ceilings are hard work. Shown stenciling the ceiling of a building in Sacramento, California *(left)*, the border of which is shown in closeup on the opposite page, Boyce allows that such work "develops incredible muscles in your neck and upper back." In merging Victorian technique and modern materials, it also creates borders and ceilings so extraordinary that lovers of Victoriana must question how they can continue to live under white plaster ceilings alone.

The Grammar of Ornament

Reviving the lost art of painted ceilings is the singular achievement of Larry Boyce, probably America's most sought-after decorative painter. Believing that "a room without a painted ceiling is like a world without a sky," and armed with a library of Victorian pattern books as inspiration, he and his crew of skilled assistants have restored hundreds of ceilings to the bold colors and intricate designs that once delighted the nineteenth-century eye. The results are spectacular, even if, as Boyce claims modestly, "Stenciling is easy, only tedious. Anyone can do it."

When Larry Boyce designs a painted ceiling for a period room, he begins with the choice of colors, anywhere from three to twelve tints, and with the selection of designs, chosen from historic pattern books. Once the selected patterns are enlarged to a size in scale with the room to be decorated, stencils are cut from plastic sheets, which are then aligned and arranged in sequence according to color. Even the most simple ceiling can thus require the stenciling of the same pattern hundreds of times, and more complex designs call for the overlay of still more repeated patterns.

"Victorian with a vengeance" is the way Boyce describes the bedroom ceiling *(left)* he painted for Richard Reutlinger's late-nineteenth-century house in San Francisco. "Exuberant Victorian, just like Larry," is the way the delighted owner prefers to describe it. Using an elaborate Eastlake pattern in keeping with the style of the house, Boyce and two assistants worked for six and one-half weeks on the project, which ultimately required 2,300 stencil applications and 980 man-hours to complete.

Details of Boyce's work *(opposite page)* reveal not only the complex beauty of Victorian patterns and their full embodiment in exuberant color, but the lush polychromed potentiality of simple molding when it yields to the magic of an artist's brush.

Artful Imitation

Graining and marbling, the cosmetic arts of making ordinary materials appear to be costly woods and marble, were skillfully practiced throughout the Victorian era, both in the home, where every professional house painter was expert in the techniques of graining softwood doors into rich-veined "portals," and in the factories, where wooden clocks and slate mantels were transformed into "adamantine" timekeepers and "verde antique" chimney pieces. Opinions on this artful fakery were about equally divided, with tastemakers like A. J. Downing and Daniel Atwood recommending it and Charles L. Eastlake branding it "an objectionable and pretentious deceit, which cannot be excused even on the ground of economy."

ESTABLISHED 1853.

KEYSTONE

SLATE MANTEL AND SLATE WORKS,

1210 Ridge Avenue.

AND

1211 and 1213 Spring Garden Street,

PHILADELPHIA.

WILSON & MILLER.

Mantels in Imitation of Spanish, Verde Antique, Egyptian, or any other Marble

Opposite page: The columns of a turn-of-the-century wooden clock are painted to resemble marble. After "overcoming the prejudices" of its snobbish critics, the Keystone Slate Mantel and Slate Works claimed in 1872 that its "slate mantel has established its reputation in the community."

The marbleized slate mantels in the double parlor of the William Case House, Pittstown, New Jersey *(above, right)*, replaced simple wooden mantels in the 1890s. The front doors of a ranch manager's house in Chugwater, Wyoming, are grained to simulate burled walnut.

7

FURNITURE

Opposite page: The front parlor of the Andrew Low House in Savannah, Georgia, is one of the most handsomely furnished period rooms in America. The c. 1848 residence on Lafayette Square, built for a cotton merchant, is now the headquarters of the National Society of Colonial Dames of America in the State of Georgia. In the 1970s the organization arranged for the refurbishing of the town house by Edward Vason Jones. Among the fine pieces is a Rococo Revival *méridienne,* and an English piano, c. 1810.

Finding just the right furniture for a Victorian-style room can be a richly rewarding experience. But be forewarned. It takes time and a generous supply of patience. The gracefully carved rosewood side chair discovered in a dim corner of the neighborhood antique shop may have no evident mate, and several years could pass before you find the right piece to use with it in the dining room. If a towering Renaissance Revival bedstead is your heart's desire, be prepared to have the side rails replaced with longer ones, and a custom box spring and mattress set made up. An antique dealer or an interior designer may be able to provide many useful tips and services, but, in the end, the decisions will still be yours as to what kind of furniture is to be used and how it is to be displayed.

The discovery that there were extremely accomplished Victorian furniture makers is a recent one. The public had been enamored of the so-called Colonial style since the turn of the century when the late-Victorians virtually reinvented it. Now the image of a dusty, cluttered nineteenth-century parlor—a veritable chamber of clunky, carved horrors—has died away. So much that was once thought to be Colonial is seen in a proper Victorian light: the painted Hitchcock chair, a scrolled pedestal-base card table, a pine nightstand with spool-turned legs are actually Victorian. And now, also, the masterpieces of such nineteenth-century cabinetmakers as John Belter, Alexander Roux, John Jelliff, and Christian Herter are pursued with the same passion devoted earlier to the American imitators of Sheraton and Hepplewhite. The Victorian marketplace in furniture, however, is

far from being overcrowded or depleted in stock. Because so much well-designed and executed furniture was produced in workshops and factories during the nineteenth century, the supply of everyday pieces is practically endless. The variety of forms, materials, and decorative motifs is amazingly diverse. Golden-oak center tables, black-walnut whatnots, and laminated Bentwood rockers should only tempt one to further explore the rich resources of the imaginative Victorian decades.

Furnishing a period room calls for as much appreciation of color and form as the study of antique settings. Although antique pieces in all the Victorian styles shown in the following pages are still available, decorating in only one historic style may not bring happy results in the private home. Museum settings in which time has stopped should be used only for the lessons in period taste they provide. For example, the parlor of the Park-McCullough House *(opposite page)* is colorfully furnished with a set of Turkish-style pieces from the 1870s. The approach taken by the curator of this house museum is well-documented and the result very pleasing. To live with such studied elegance at home is another matter. The owners of the Little Rock, Arkansas, Hanger House *(below)* have slowly refurbished their 1889 parlor. Antiques representative of several decades of Victorian taste are mixed together; even a comfortable modern sofa is used. This is a period room that a family can truly enjoy and appreciate.

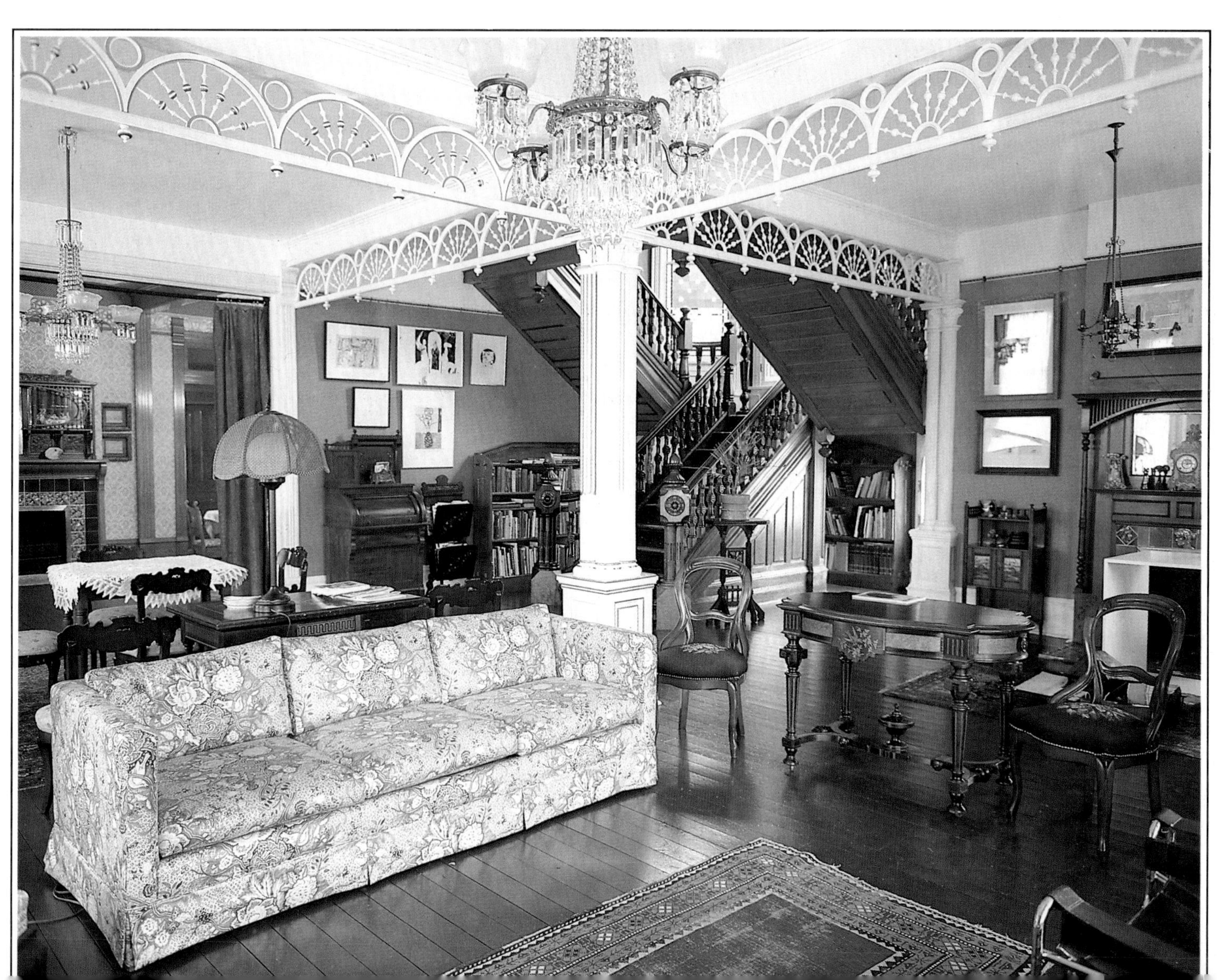

The Principal Furniture Styles

TRANSITIONAL VICTORIAN

The emergence of a distinctive Victorian furniture form came slowly during the 1830s and '40s. There was a gradual movement away from chaste neoclassical ornamentation toward a more ornate interpretation of the classical form. This can be seen in such details as the turned legs of mahogany chests of drawers and armchairs (as opposed to the earlier simpler sword-like legs) and in more decorative carving of chair splats and rails.

GOTHIC REVIVAL

Gothic furniture was an acquired taste in the 1830s and '40s, and, because it was not widely produced, examples are rare today. A. J. Downing, the leading proponent of Gothic architecture and design, doubted that the furniture would ever attain popularity: "It is too elaborately Gothic—with the same high-pointed arches, crockets, and carving usually seen in the front of some cathedral." But it did survive, as a unique example of the romantic imagination.

ROCOCO REVIVAL

The gracefully curving lines of Rococo Revival furniture of the 1840s through the '60s reflect the public fascination with French style, in particular, Louis XV. The oval and scroll forms appear again and again in chairs, sofas, beds, tables, and dressers. Black walnut and various other hardwoods such as cherry and rosewood were shaped with an eye to the opulent effect. Deep, narrow moldings and carved ornamentation often outline the forms, endowing them with a special richness. John Belter (1804-63) is the acknowledged master of the style, and it was he who invented a process for laminating wood.

COTTAGE STYLE

In sharp contrast to the high-style designs imitating French furniture are the many forms of Cottage furniture. Popular from the 1840s until late in the century, Cottage furniture was intended for the simple country house, but was used everywhere except in the most formal settings. Often of black walnut, maple, or pine, Cottage furniture is usually distinguished by straightforward lines and spool turnings. Chairs and tables are often ornamented with paint or stenciling rather than with carving. This is seen most markedly in the mass-produced chairs of Lambert Hitchcock, first manufactured in the pre-Civil War period and imitated ever since. Well-made and appropriate today in almost all nineteenth-century period rooms, Cottage pieces are true American country antiques well worth searching for.

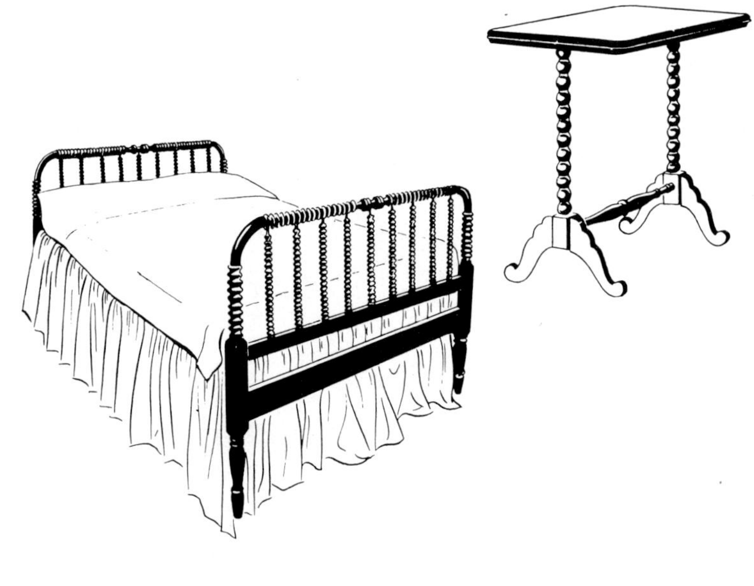

RENAISSANCE REVIVAL

Massive, somewhat boxy chairs, tables, beds, cabinets, and sideboards with elaborate ornamentation embody the Renaissance Revival style. Many of the pieces incorporate such ornamental detailing as marquetry, inlay, and applied moldings. Finials and cresting are used, and slabs of colored marble are sometimes employed for tops and shelving. So imposing are many of the forms that, when arranged in a room setting, they appear to have been built in place. Yet most of these architectural pieces were factory-assembled in Grand Rapids or other furniture-making centers. Popular from the late 1850s through the '70s, Renaissance Revival furniture mirrored the taste of contemporary Europe. It is a style just beginning to be appreciated anew.

EASTLAKE STYLE

Reacting to the heavy ornamentation of the various revival styles popular from the 1840s, Charles L. Eastlake proposed a more "honest," straightforward approach to furniture design. The English designer and architect's *Hints on Household Taste* went through many American printings in the 1870s and '80s. Incised rather than carved decoration and angular rather than curved lines distinguish the oak and walnut pieces of his inspiration.

CLASSICAL REVIVAL

Late-nineteenth-century bedroom and parlor sets in the style of Louis XVI were everything that Renaissance Revival furniture was not—light, carved, and gilded, and, in seating furniture, deeply upholstered. In an aristocratic thumbing of the nose at the prevalent taste for bulky pieces, the doyenne of European elegance, Edith Wharton, extolled in *The Decoration of Houses* (1897) the eighteenth-century French "small *meubles,* in which beauty of design and workmanship were joined to simplicity and convenience."

MIXING AND MATCHING

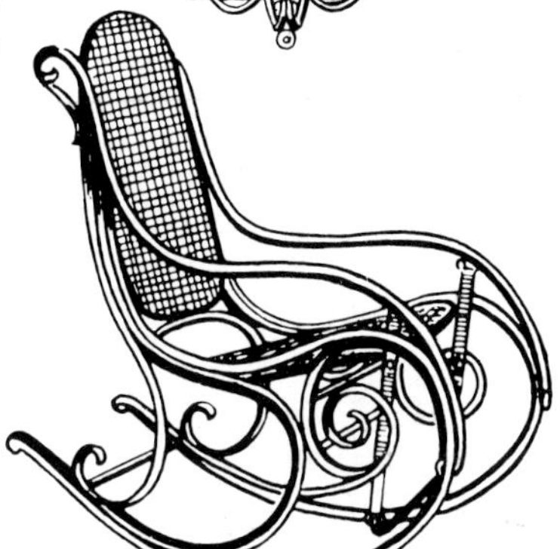

As in any period, the average Victorian home was furnished in a mixture of furniture styles. Throughout the 1800s, such familiar Colonial forms as the Windsor chair and the wing chair found useful places in the house. The parlor was the one room that was most often refurbished with fashionable new pieces from generation to generation. The fashion for decorating all rooms *en suite*—that is, with matching furniture—was a luxury that few Americans could afford. Outside of the parlor, the choice of furnishings might be potluck—a grouping of wicker pieces, a Bentwood rocker, a caned ladderback, an ottoman or Morris chair, iron and brass bedsteads and stands. The Victorians were just as likely as we are today to choose comfort and convenience over style.

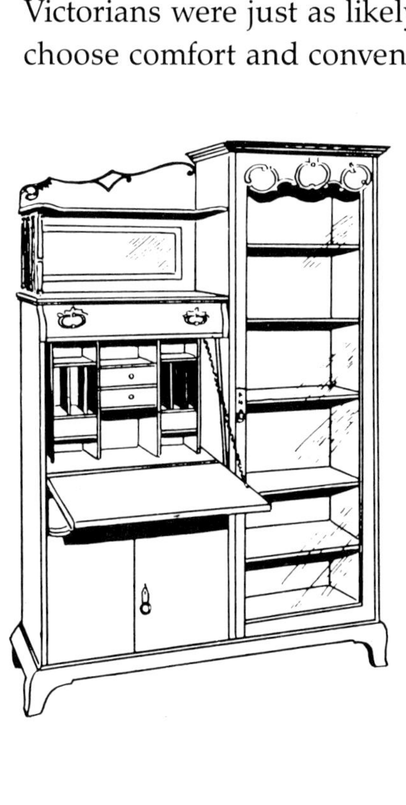

The Parlor

Step back in time for a moment to the Victorian parlor. This is the "best" room, the place where the tone, the style of the residence, is set. It is the room in which the finest a family has to offer is expressed in furniture and appointments, a place, in the words of a late-Victorian enthusiast, "full of beauty and brightness, testifying at once to the large and generous hospitality, as well as to the taste and wise discrimination of the queen-mistress who reigns over the realm of which this is the state chamber." Children sometimes find the parlor a rather forbidding realm, but they learn to take their place in it—upon the high-backed sofa, before the upright piano, or even behind the flowing damask drapes. The principal pieces of seating furniture are upholstered and, in the summer months, slipcovered or draped to ward off the effects of the sun. A center table serves as a con-

Parlors from three different periods of the nineteenth century illustrate the changes in furnishings which occurred from decade to decade. The William A. Farnsworth House, Rockland, Maine *(above, left)* was built c. 1854 in the Greek Revival style. It has been preserved as a museum with all of its lavish furnishings, including sets of Gothic Revival and Rococo Revival side chairs. Montauk *(left)*, the Clermont, Iowa, home of Governor William Larrabee, was built in the Italianate style in 1874. Visible in one corner of the parlor are two pieces of an elegant Renaissance Revival set and a much simpler Cottage-style rocking chair. On the opposite page is a typically eclectic 1890s parlor, the room carefully arranged for the visiting photographer. The heavily upholstered and draped pieces barely look touched by human hands.

From the 1840s to the '70s, Rococo Revival furniture remained fashionable in the homes of successful businessmen and political figures. Only late in this period was the relatively simple curvilinear style to be replaced in favor by the more angular and ornate Renaissance Revival. Rococo Revival and early Renaissance Revival pieces look "right" in the parlors illustrated here because they are essentially in harmony with the general architectural décor of the rooms themselves.

At the right is a parlor in the Cameron-Stanford House, Oakland, California, an Italianate mansion now a museum. The graceful matching love seats are similar to thousands produced in the mid-1800s. On the opposite page, upper left, is a view of the connecting parlor and library of the General Grenville M. Dodge House, Council Bluffs, Iowa, with a walnut Rococo Revival parlor set still in place. The house, built in 1869-70, has woodwork and built-in walnut appointments throughout its first floor. Illustrated below it is the Patrick Barry House parlor and library. Built in 1855-57, the Rochester, New York, mansion has many of its original Rococo Revival furnishings. At upper right is the parlor of Fort Hill, Clemson, South Carolina, the home of John C. Calhoun from 1825 to 1850. It is furnished with complementary pieces of that period. Below the Calhoun mansion is another view of Montauk (see page 118), built in 1874, and furnished with early Renaissance Revival pieces.

venient place for books and a reading lamp. All of the furniture is arranged in relation to the central architectural feature of the room, the hearth or its stove, with the possible exception of a bookcase or a desk tucked away in a quiet corner. The parlor is the place for reading after supper, peaceful games in the evening, formal socializing, and Sunday devotions.

In the post-Civil War period, the average Victorian parlor became more and more elaborate in furnishings and ornamentation. The terms "salon" and "drawing room" came into increasing use among the well-to-do to describe the most formal room of the house. Above all, the parlor became the place for the display of fine art, such as portraits and genre paintings, and sculptural objects, such as ornamental vases and busts. One corner might contain space for a whatnot, étagère, or glass French cabinet in which prized pieces of china, silver, and glass could be displayed. Except in the Classical Revival drawing room of the turn of the century, the center table remained in place. In addition there were occasional tables for lamps, stands such as the Turkish tabouret, and often a delicate tray or tea table from which guests were served. The drawing room, as it was called, of the James Whitcomb Riley House in Indianapolis, Indiana *(right)*, is typical of stylish residences of the late 1870s. The room is comfortably furnished with well-upholstered and fringed chairs and sofa in the exotic Turkish style of the 1880s. A chair of this type, Clarence Cook wrote in *The House Beautiful* (1878), "is so pretty to look at, that one forgets to sit down in it. . . ." A hostess could hardly have asked for a more double-edged remark.

Deep-cushioned and richly upholstered parlor furniture contributed to an air of ease. The tête-à-tête, as illustrated above, was meant to encourage the sharing of intimacies, albeit with some twisting of necks. The unusual piece fills a cosy corner in the parlor of the 1889 Long-Waterman House, San Diego, California. By the next decade, the tête-à-tête and such extravagant furniture pieces as the ottoman were falling into disfavor among the wealthy and those imbued with the art craftsman's aesthetic. Robert Machek, a gifted Austrian woodworker, preferred much cleaner lines for the parlor furniture *(left)* in the home he built for himself in Milwaukee, Wisconsin, in 1894. Millionaire Christian Heurich chose the newly fashionable Classical Revival style for the drawing room furnishings of his 1892 Washington, D.C., mansion *(above, left)*.

The Hall

The Victorian hall is much more than a passageway between rooms. Usually of wider proportions than its modern equivalent, the hall provides useful auxilliary space for family living. The front hall or entry is, in addition, the place where guests are welcomed and much of the paraphernalia of the outdoors arranged. Hall trees or stands are quaint but useful repositories of coats, overshoes, umbrellas, and hats. Several chairs may be positioned along the walls to provide comfortable seating for the removal or donning of outside apparel. Along the wall near the front door is often a pier table or console where it was once the practice to leave cards or messages of greeting. Upstairs, the hall may be furnished with comfortable chairs and a sofa, the furniture group forming a pleasant nook for reading or needlework. With a lively wallpaper and pleasant lighting, both upper and lower halls can be attractive features of the house.

The second-floor hall of the George H. Corliss House in Providence, Rhode Island, is sufficiently wide to function as a pleasant sitting room and gallery of family portraits. Seen at the right is the main entry hall of Roselawn, the Henry C. Bowen mansion in Woodstock, Connecticut. Built in 1846, the house still contains Gothic Revival furniture designed by architect Joseph Wells, including the side chair, table, and hall stand with their marked tracery. Bowen, a noted abolitionist and publisher, greeted many famous guests in this front hall, among them all the U.S. presidents from Grant to McKinley.

A sweeping staircase dominates the entry hall of Louisville, Kentucky's 1868 Ronald-Brennan House *(opposite page)*. Yet there is still room for a massive Renaissance Revival étagère, a matching hall stand, and a grandfather's clock.

Hall stands or trees are colorful and useful Victorian antiques. The two models shown opposite feature mirrors, pegs for hanging wraps, space for overshoes, and umbrella rails.

The Dining Room

A room for formal dining in the average middle-class house came into its own in the nineteenth century. Before this time—except in great Georgian Colonial mansions or Federal town houses—meals were served in a parlor, kitchen, and wherever else space might allow. The Victorian housewife demanded a separate room for family dining and entertaining, and while it might be used only on Sunday or for dinner parties, the room became established as an essential part of a proper Victorian residence. The dining room was a social extension of the parlor, a second "best" room filled with fine furniture and objects of vertu. An elegant dining room suite, consisting of a table, matching chairs, and a commode or sideboard of some sort, was the dream of every homeowner. Tables that could be extended with the use of extra leaves were a specialty of the Victorian furniture maker. An extraordinary number of these heavy oak and mahogany dining tables with pedestal bases or thick and fluted legs are to be found today in antique shops and auction galleries. A matching set of chairs is more difficult to come by, but from the thousands of different styles produced, and which still survive, a selection of complementary pieces can be put together.

Ornately carved sideboards and serving cabinets were frequently custom-made pieces intended to occupy a special place within the dining room. The example illustrated at the left is from the home of famed Milwaukee brewer Alfred Uihlein. Like many such pieces, it was built as a permanent part of the room, where it remained until the 1887 mansion was demolished in the 1970s. Designed for show, it also served a practical use as a place to store and display serving dishes and various other fine accoutrements.

America's wealthiest Victorian families often turned to European craftsmen for their best furnishings. Well-traveled and possessed of nearly limitless means, these aristocrats entertained on a lavish scale equal to that of Paris or London. The Wetmores were one such American Social Register family, and the dining salon of their Newport, Rhode Island, summer house, Chateau-sur-Mer *(left)*, testifies both to their taste and their wealth. The mansion was built on Bellevue Avenue in 1851-52 and almost totally redesigned by Richard Morris Hunt in the 1870s. The burl-walnut paneled dining room was installed in 1877-78 and is the work of Luigi Frullini of Florence in the then-popular Renaissance Revival style. The set of chairs is upholstered in the same tooled leather design as that used on the walls. This room, as well as other important areas of the mansion, has been refurbished recently by the Preservation Society of Newport County.

The dining room of the Tacon-Gordon House, Mobile, Alabama *(left)*, is far less imposing than that of Chateau-sur-Mer, but no less stylish for its time. A Colonial Revival home of the turn of the century, it is furnished in keeping with the current fashion for simpler, less "European" antiques. The Hepplewhite-style chairs and the drop-leaf table are as English as they are American, but in the 1890s and early 1900s such pieces were considered as indubitably American as George and Martha Washington.

The actual number of pieces of furniture found in most Victorian dining rooms is very small in comparison to the multitude of objects displayed in the parlor or master bedroom. The dining room, the most specialized space in the house, serves only one function, to provide a graceful setting for meals. This functional purpose is well-illustrated in the spare and strikingly beautiful dining room of Glessner House *(left)*. H. H. Richardson's landmark Romanesque residence was designed for Chicago businessman John J. Glessner in 1886. The finest furniture craftsmen were employed in the production of pieces with solid but flowing sculptured lines which anticipate the Art Nouveau style. The distinctive dining room chairs were designed by Charles Coolidge, one of Richardson's assistants and successors.

The marked horizontality of the sophisticated urban craftsman's work of the 1880s contrasts sharply with that of the earlier Renaissance Revival artist in wood. While both styles emphasize mass, the thrust of the earlier style is vertical, almost pyramidal. As seen in the dining room of the Ronald-Brennan House, Louisville, Kentucky *(left)*, the ornate pieces are designed to attract the eye upward to the fanciful cresting. A dining room set of this type and quality is unusual to find intact today. Because of a foreshortening in the photograph, the room appears smaller than it actually is. The space easily accommodates a set of eight chairs, two sideboards, dining table, and glass cabinet.

The essential functional character of the late-Victorian dining room is readily apparent in a Hudson, New York, Colonial Revival town house *(left)*. Except for the extension table and chairs, everything is built in place. With so much free space, it is an easy task to add yet another leaf to the table for guests. The use of one primary material—oak—helps to relate the few furnishings to each other. The table, built especially for the room, has an edge molding of the same egg and dart design as the handsomely paneled woodwork and cabinets. The classical entablature crowning the door frame and the surround of the recessed cabinet, as well as the broken scroll pediments of the chairs, are inspired high-style Colonial Revival flourishes.

The early Victorians were hardly less fastidious in their dining room appointments. If there is, indeed, a rule to be followed in decorating such rooms from the 1840s or '50s, it would be—keep it simple. Dining room suites were available at the time, but not at all commonly used. In the Spartan room shown at the left, early-nineteenth-century splat-back armchairs surround a drop-leaf, gateleg table. The lazy Susan is a useful device on any circular dining table and a convenient perch for a caster set.

The Bedroom

Although outward forms changed dramatically through the years, the fundamental elements of bedroom furnishings remained remarkably constant during the Victorian era. After years of unrivaled popularity, the traditional American fourposter was gradually replaced in many prosperous homes by elaborately carved Rococo Revival and Renaissance Revival bedsteads in black walnut, rosewood, and grained imitations of these expensive woods. Such monumental pieces, often with towering headboards, were usually accompanied by other furniture in a suite specially purchased for the bedroom that included a bureau, wardrobe, washstand, nightstand, rocker, and love seat or chaise longue. Marble tops on some of the pieces provided protection against the soapy residue of washbasins. Suites of varying quality and cost were first offered widely in the 1840s, and some, made of pine, were readily affordable by the average family. Such varnished or painted pieces were known as Cottage suites and became a staple of nineteenth-century manufacturers, even as bedsteads in iron and brass increased in popularity toward the end of the century.

Throughout the Victorian era, the bedroom was seen increasingly as a place of comfortable repose, a room not only for sleep, but for a nap on a chaise or for relaxing contemplation in a cozy rocking chair. Contemporary sentimentalism saw the bedroom as the "mother's room," a term apostrophized in *Beautiful Homes* (1878), by Henry T. Williams and Mrs. C. S. Jones, as "that most delightful retreat, that sacred casket in which are enshrined the smiles and tears of childhood's hour, the joys and sorrows of youthful days, the confessions and confidences of maturer years, all poured into the fond mother's ear and hallowed by her admonitions and prayers."

Photographed in the 1890s, the master bedroom of the Barber House in Washington, D.C. *(opposite page)*, reveals all the feminine requirements of a comfortable "mother's room." A chaise is placed at the foot of the bedstead, where instead of the blanket chest so beloved of historic home restorers, it almost always appears in documentary photographs. A rocking chair and a platform rocker provide additional comfort.

A monumental suite of Renaissance Revival furniture fills one of the bedrooms of Washington, D.C.'s Blair House *(left)*. Acquired long after the residence was erected in the 1820s, the suite was no doubt a fashionable addition to the household even though its massive bulk would be far more in scale with the high-ceilinged rooms of Italianate or Second Empire houses contemporaneous with Renaissance Revival furniture.

In addition to its obvious utility, furniture has always been used to establish a stylistic flavor, an impression of fashionable good taste. According to A. J. Downing, "furniture in good taste is characterized by its being designed in accordance with certain recognized styles, and intended to accord with apartments in the same style." Yet, as documentary photographs reveal, the harmony of style held to be ideal was rarely achieved. Rather, furnishings were generally eclectic throughout the Victorian era and were representative of at least several generations. Even when building a new house, a family was more than likely to carry along treasured pieces from its old residence. Rather than stylistic unity, the guideline for furnishing a period room should be harmony between scale, material, and quality of workmanship.

The bedrooms at the right illustrate this principle. Although the high ceilings of the Second-Empire Park-McCullough House in North Bennington, Vermont, are suitable for massive Renaissance Revival furniture, the airy rattan pieces and brass bedstead, typical of turn-of-the-century furnishings, are equally suitable because they work harmoniously with one another. Matching oak beds define the children's bedroom of the Hanger House, Little Rock, Arkansas, as impeccably Victorian in form. Modern art does not at all detract from the decorative harmony of the space. In fact, it gives the room a definite character that sets it apart from many period rooms that are artificially frozen in time.

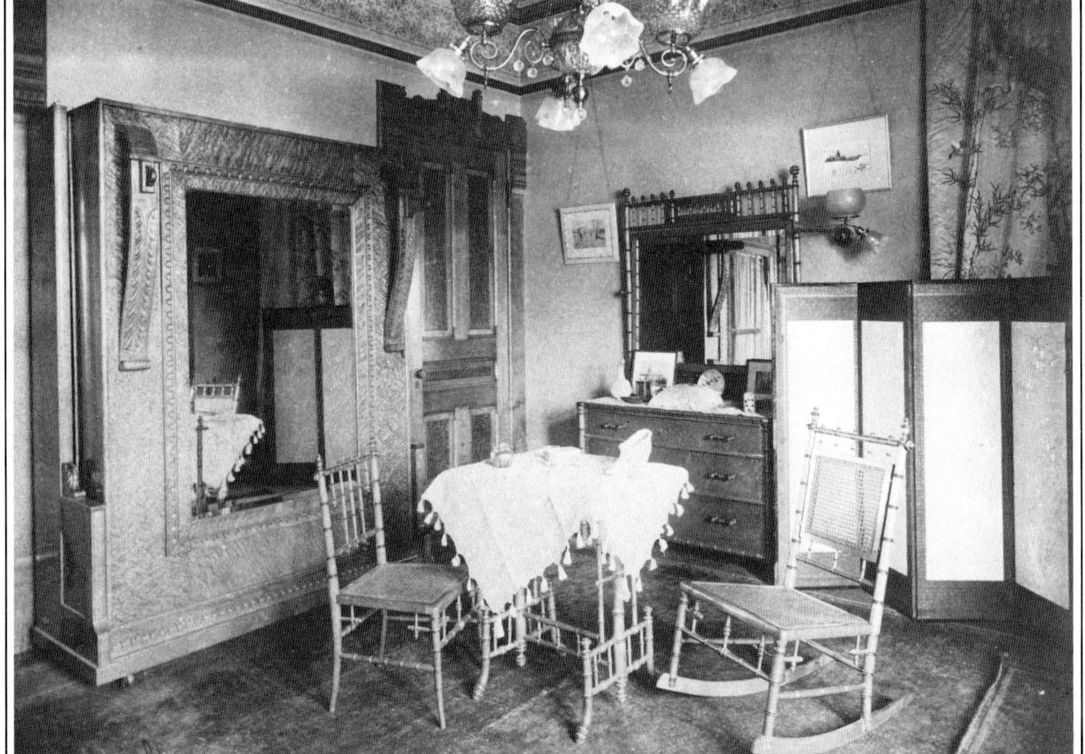

Few Victorians, even if they could afford to do so, furnished their bedrooms with contemporaneous pieces. Although the James Whitcomb Riley House was built in 1872, the poet's bedroom, photographed in 1900 *(above)*, was furnished with a chamber suite of the 1850s.

With the development of the mass-produced portable bed *(left)*, spare bedrooms could easily double as informal sitting rooms, or lodgers could be made comfortable in their own one-room suites. In the 1890s, Sears offered similar folding beds that weighed "only 250 pounds."

The Bath

Historians are fond of listing the wondrous succession of inventions that changed the face of Victorian America—the telegraph, the telephone, the incandescent bulb. But an even better case for immortality might be claimed by an innovation far more important in its impact on everyday life. To think of noxious privies, inconvenient dirt closets, or the weekly visit of the public cart to remove "night soil," is to recognize the marvel of indoor plumbing and its importance to the Victorian home. At first the province of the rich, plumbing eventually became available to people of more modest means. Their bathrooms—lined with tiles or wainscoted with wood, illuminated during the day by stained-glass windows and at night by gas—contained ornamental fixtures once considered hopelessly passé but now deemed to have character and grace. Only someone who has bathed in a Victorian tub knows what nineteenth-century luxury can be.

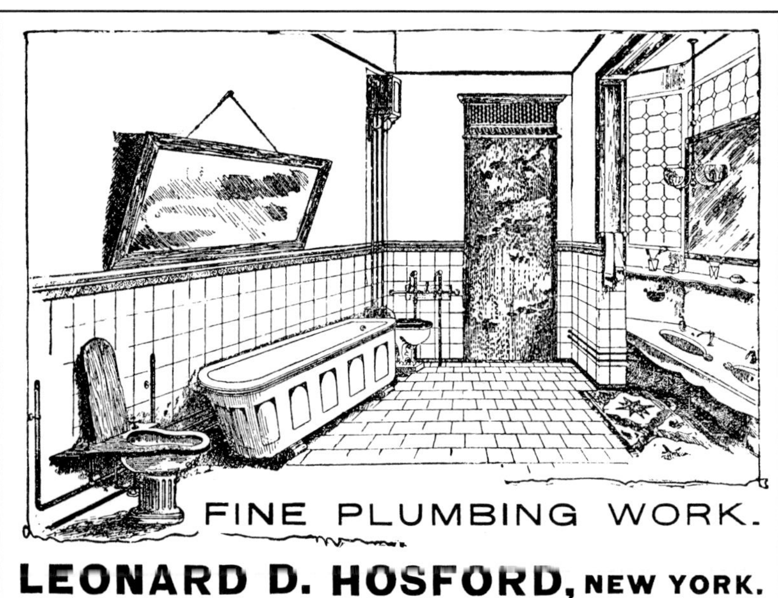

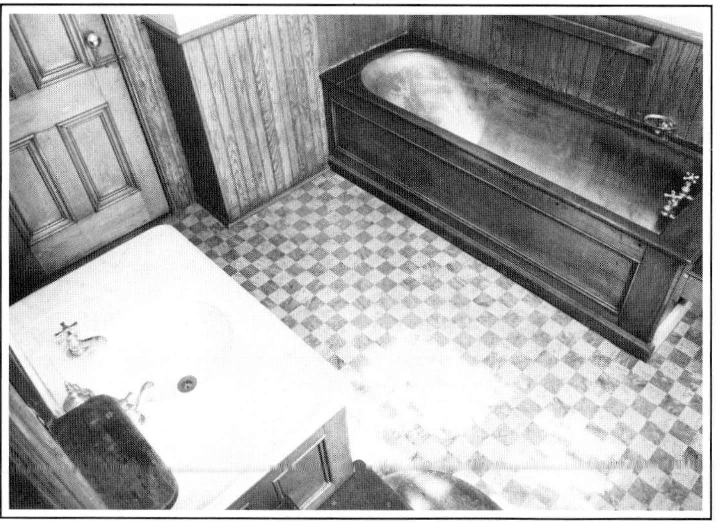

The 1893 advertisement on the opposite page, with its tiled walls and unenclosed plumbing fixtures, is in sharp relief to all the other late-Victorian bathrooms pictured here. Since the American bathroom was a room without any precedent in domestic history, a debate raged between those who treated the room traditionally—as a space to be papered and wainscoted and furnished with handsome cabinets that disguised the fixtures—and those who were "modern" and influenced by a growing army of scientific "home economists." The battle cry of the latter might very well have been, "Tile or die!" "The exposed tub and exposed plumbing," wrote one expert in 1894, "all make for health and cleanliness. If decoration is to be used in the bathroom, forego it and put the money in tiles. Wallpaper is not desirable in a bathroom. Nor is wood-paneling, which only tempts the prolific waterbug."

Today it's possible to have it either way—tile or wood—and without the threat of germs or bugs. Waterproof papers, unknown to the Victorians, can complement wainscoting and cabinetry treated to withstand moisture. While it might be difficult to reproduce exactly the high-style bathrooms illustrated here, the combined talents of antique or reproduction plumbing dealers and millwork suppliers can approximate the look with ease. (What the world needs now is a manufacturer to reproduce the 1893 tub on the right, with its row of brass controls, including two that make waves.)

Sanctum Sanctorum

Long before the advent of the ubiquitous family room, there was a place where the head of a prosperous household might sneak away for an hour or two, if for nothing more than the innocent reading of the evening newspaper. Men of lesser means escaped the tyranny of the parlor by moving to the stoop or, in colder weather, the corner bar; the wealthy man resorted to the den or library. Not that other members of the household were not allowed inside such a sanctum sanctorum. There are many photographic records of proper Victorian ladies enjoying the smoky precincts of a den or cueing up the ball at a game of billiards in an attic room. But the den, library, office, smoking room, or study was basically a habitat for gentlemen, and decorated and furnished accordingly. Depending upon its use, the room might contain built-in shelving for books, a smoking stand, a liquor cabinet, and a desk or center table for cards. Almost always there were wide-bodied, well-cushioned chairs for relaxation.

The various proprietors of Lyndhurst, most notably tycoon Jay Gould, surely enjoyed the amenities of the mansion, including the dignified library *(above, right)*. The Gothic Revival estate in Tarrytown, New York, was designed by Alexander Jackson Davis and Ithiel Town and completed in 1838. Gould became its owner in 1880, and the furnishings of the room reflect this later period. With its amply proportioned chairs and neatly appointed table, this was a room worthy of quiet contemplation. The office *(right)* was, undoubtedly, a busier place. It is furnished with a splendid all-purpose Wooten desk. This extraordinary contraption, priceless today, was patented in 1874 by William S. Wooten and appealed to such well-organized men of lavish means as John D. Rockefeller and Joseph Pulitzer.

The measured, dignified style of life enjoyed by the two principal proprietors of the Ronald-Brennan House, Louisville, Kentucky, is summarized in the view of the library *(above, left)*. Francis Ronald, a wholesale tobacco merchant, had the house built in 1868; it was later the residence of Thomas Brennan, an industrialist and inventor.

We know little of J. A. St. John of Boston, but photographer Charles Currier was allowed to record his ebulliently-decorated smoking room in the 1890s *(left)*. The wicker chaise and chairs might well find a place in a hunting lodge. The only suggestions of big game, however, are found in the leonine fire screen and the horns above the overmantel. Mr. St. John, as the table testifies, was more interested in pipe dreams.

Mark Twain couldn't stand the study planned for his 1874 Hartford, Connecticut, mansion. Instead, he retreated to the billiard room on the third floor *(above)* to compose and to relax.

8

THE VICTORIAN HEARTH

Opposite page: A marble mantel with a gracefully arched opening is the focal point of one of the parlors in the Ronald-Brennan House, built in Louisville, Kentucky, in 1868. A generation later, such mantels were considered "hideous," a betrayal of classical proportions, and were widely replaced by Adamesque imitations in the Colonial Revival style.

The nineteenth-century hearth, linked as it was to the vicissitudes of Victorian heating technology, was constantly in flux. The owners of a single house built in 1850 might have begun with a graceful marble mantel in the parlor, replaced it with a monumental wooden mantel in the '70s, boarded up the opening and vented a stove pipe through it in the '80s, and installed a hot-water radiator in front of it in the '90s. This forward march of progress, from fireplace to stove to central heat, means, of course, a wide range of options for anyone decorating in the Victorian style since all three heating modes are "proper" for the nineteenth-century interior. But even though a central source of heat meant that there was no longer a need for fireplaces, even though some houses built in the late 1800s dispensed with fireplaces altogether, the custom of including a mantel—at least in the parlor—survived the advance of heating technology. Although essentially ornamental, the fireplace remained the focal point of a formal room's composition. The furnishings and the very arrangement of furniture in such rooms were related to the position of the fireplace, even after it had ceased to serve a functional purpose. The family hearth is such a strong symbol of domesticity in America that even the fake fireplace found in many late-Victorian homes was thought to radiate comfort to those surrounding it.

"But what on earth is half so dear—so longed for—as the hearth of home?" asked Emily Brontë, that most unsentimental of Victorian writers. The answer to her rhetorical question is nothing—nothing at all. The hearth was as central to Victorian notions of warmth and comfort as it is to ours in the energy-worried present.

The Fireplace

"A fire-place goes farther than anything else in giving to a room character and beauty. Every parlor, dining-room, and nursery, at least, should have one. In the cool weather of spring and fall, when the morning and evening air is a little sharp, or when a long cold rain-storm is making everything damp, moist, and uncomfortable, there is nothing more delightful, both for old and young, than a brisk fire upon an open hearth. With what beautiful rosy light and a gentle warmth, it fills a room, and how it laughs and dances and seems to say to every one, 'be glad with me!' And then, aside from its home-like beauty and good cheer, the depressing chills and miasma, the floating seeds of disease, will be seized by its friendly flames and whirled up the chimney before they have time to lay a finger on us."

Sarah J. Hale
Godey's Lady's Book (1870)

Marble mantels, with gracefully-curved openings, were in vogue between the 1840s and the 1860s and to modern eyes appear, like the mantelpiece above, particularly attractive in their handsome simplicity. They were produced in such abundance, however, that they soon were deemed unfashionable, as wooden mantels, ever more elaborate, grew in favor. Novelist Edith Wharton, who with Ogden Codman, Jr., called for a return to classical proportions in *The Decoration of Houses* (1897), suggested that those who could afford it should discard their "hideous" mantels for new ones "of good design." The Classical Revival mantel at the right was one contemporary example of "good design," one that Mrs. Wharton would have applauded.

Standing at the symbolic and physical center of nearly every Victorian parlor was the fireplace mantel. A functional element in most homes until the end of the century, the fireplace determined in large part how a room was used and its furniture arranged. As Wharton and Codman put it, "The fireplace must be the focus of every rational scheme of arrangement." The mantel, of course, whether simple or ornate, set the tone of the entire room. The mantels shown here can only suggest the variety of Victorian mantelpieces and the possibilities inherent in working wood and marble.

The Hearthside Stove

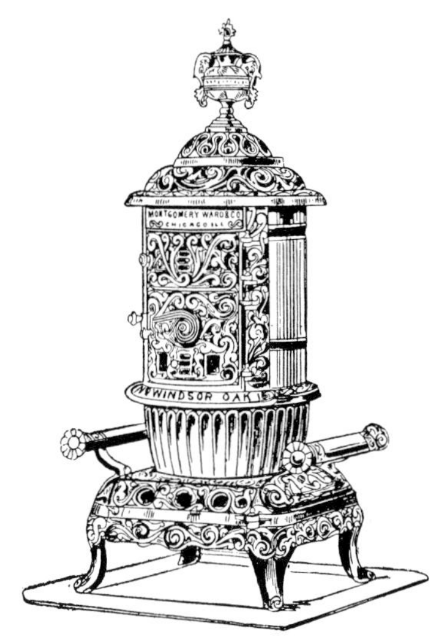

When in 1880 Mark Twain came to write the chapter of his *Life on the Mississippi* entitled "The House Beautiful," he waxed nostalgic for the bygone day of the open fireplace and its crackling flames instead of a "polished airtight stove (new and deadly invention), with pipe passing through a board which closes up the discarded good old fireplace." The famous writer could afford to be nostalgic. He was a wealthy man. And his fireplace-filled mansion was fitted with central heat.

Most Victorians were not quite so fortunate. When cast-iron stoves, vastly improved since the days of Benjamin Franklin, came within the means of most middle-class Americans after 1850, they were immediately seen as an economic blessing. No longer did the inefficient fireplace have to be fed an endless supply of costly fuel. Staying warm took precedence over literary charm.

Opposite page: The efficiency of American railroads in the late nineteenth century enabled mail-order houses to carry on a thriving business in household stoves even though a large ten-plate parlor stove weighed almost half a ton. Stoves of various types from the 1895 Montgomery Ward catalogue and the Sears, Roebuck catalogue of two years later are pictured clockwise from upper right: "Windsor Oak," a wood-burning parlor stove; a small Elwood wood-burner suitable for bedrooms; "Ward Windsor," a self-feeding hard coal parlor stove; "Box Sunshine," a box stove for wood heating and cooking very much like the first box stoves introduced in the 1830s; a Duke cannon stove for hard or soft coal that derives its generic name from its shape; and "Gay Sunshine," with a "revertible flue" outside the stove that allowed greater radiation of heat and savings in fuel.

An 1850 cast-iron stove in the Gothic mode *(above, left)*, replaced the fireplace in the 1833 Dr. Alfred Paige House in Bethel, Vermont. The decorative finial holds water to humidify the room. A stove from the same period and made by R. & J. Wainright of Middlebury, Vermont *(above, right)* is in another bedroom of the same house. Dated 1889, a "Perfect" cast-iron stove insert *(far left)* warms the parlor of the Elliott House, Petersburg, Virginia. The "Art Jewel," like many late-Victorian parlor stoves, has isinglass windows to compensate for the loss of the cheerful glow of a fireplace fire.

Steam Heat

Although several central heating systems were patented in America by 1850, only the well-to-do could afford such luxury at first. By the 1880s, however, the mechanics of heating had been so improved, and the prices so reduced, that central heating began to appear regularly in the houses of the middle class. Given the choice between ducts for a hot-air system or pipes for a radiator system, more people chose pipes because they were easier and cheaper to install. As a result, hot-air registers, beautifully ornamented and discreetly hidden, appeared in Victorian homes less frequently than radiators that had to be displayed as prominently as furniture. While some people continue to despise the hulking presence of these cast-iron pieces, others, insisting on their considerable charms, maintain that a late-Victorian room without a radiator's friendly hiss is as empty as a period house without the ticking of a clock.

Not all radiators were simple, functional affairs, displayed unaffectedly in all their naked honesty. Those who could afford to, disguised the hissing pipes from public view. The newly-constructed dining room of Lyndhurst, Tarrytown, New York (1865), featured a magnificently decorative radiator to which an étagère was later added *(left)*. That there is no end to Victorian ingenuity is illustrated at the right.

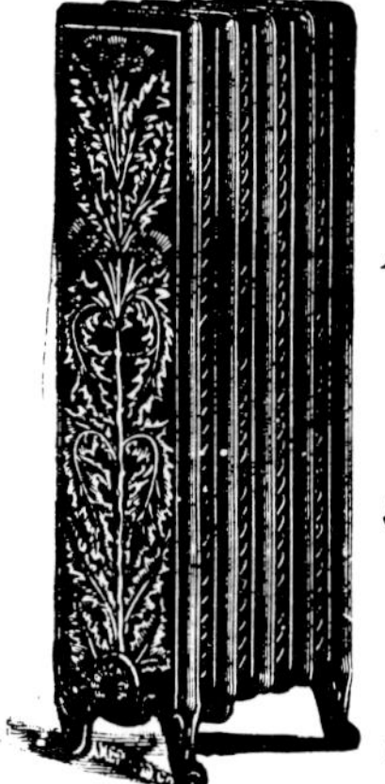

RADIATORS,

For Steam and Hot Water.

Artistic Designs, ...
Perfect Circulation,
Largest Assortment,
. . . . . . *Best Constructed.*

SIMPLE, EFFICIENT, RELIABLE

AMERICAN RADIATOR COMPANY

111 AND 113 LAKE ST., CHICAGO, ILL.

PERFECTION FLUE.

FACTORIES: **DETROIT AND BUFFALO.**

DETROIT, DINING ROOM.

New York: 92 CENTRE STREET.
Boston: 44 OLIVER STREET.
Minneapolis: 324 NORTH FIRST STREET.
St. Paul: NATIONAL GERMAN AMERICAN BANK BUILDING.

As an 1893 advertisement for the American Radiator Company proclaims, "Simple, Efficient, Reliable" radiators were frequently decorated with stamped "Artistic Designs." These designs were repeated in the semiattached covers that were sold together with the heating units. Although almost everyone today seems to paint radiators a shiny silver color, these decorative devices were usually painted much more vibrantly, with a ground in one color and the raised pattern in another, the whole intended to harmonize with the essential colors of the room.

The Kitchen Hearth

There's no use romanticizing the Victorian kitchen. Thornton Wilder might have been nostalgic for all those apple-pie smells emanating from the kitchens of *Our Town*, but he never saw the kitchen hearth from a woman's point of view. The Victorian housewife walked hundreds of miles annually just tending the appliances in her obstacle-course kitchen. A coal or wood stove was often four to five feet wide, and even taller if furnished with a high shelf. Feeding it broke the back; its heat, the spirit. A wooden icebox could measure two to three feet across; an iron sink fitted with a drying rack and a force pump to draw water from the cistern could take up nearly a whole wall. In 1879 one expert on "household management" wrote that "the kitchen is a family laboratory, and a good cook should be a chemist." In actuality, the family chemist was a combination marathon runner, workhorse, and mechanic. Cast-iron cookstoves are being manufactured once again. Only a museum curator would want one.

The stoves shown here can only suggest the variety offered the Victorian consumer. Heated by circulating hot water, the warming stove in a butler's pantry *(above, right)* was used to keep food and plates at the right temperature for serving. A Walker's range, still connected to its hot-water storage tank *(right)*, is similar, except in ornamentation, to the elevated oven range advertised by John Q. A. Butler in 1876 *(opposite page)* and a far cry from the simpler cookstove below it advertised in 1869. The remaining ranges—"Home Sunshine"—and "Family Sunshine"—are two of many offered in the 1897 Sears, Roebuck catalogue. The latter, with a horizontal boiler above the cooking shelf, weighed three-quarters of a ton.

The Grand Central Elevated Oven Range,

The Latest and Best!

FOUR SIZES, Nos. 2, 3, 4 and 5.

JOHN Q. A. BUTLER,

DIGHTON FURNACE COMPANY

COOKING, OFFICE, AND PARLOR STOVES.

Ornamental Tiles

A fireplace hearth paved with encaustic tiles in patterns of earthy brown or ochre, rich red or brilliant blue, seems almost quintessentially Victorian. Yet the widespread use of tiles for hearth and fireplace facing was not possible until after 1880, when American manufacturers first challenged the monopoly of European suppliers. The popularity of American-made tile corresponded with that of the wooden mantelpiece. Of the fire-retardant materials deemed necessary to separate mantel, floor, and firebox, tile was considered not only more attractive than brick, but also far easier to clean.

The development of American mass-produced tiles corresponded not only with the popularity of wooden mantelpieces, but with the first stirrings in this country of the Arts and Crafts movement, which saw tile as a source of color, beauty, and utility in the domestic interior. By the turn of the century, the sale of American tile far outstripped European imports, and at least thirty companies flourished to meet the demand.

A wooden mantel in the 1887 Alfred Uihlein House, Milwaukee, Wisconsin *(opposite page),* illustrates the contemporary use of decorative tiles for fireplace siding and for hearths. The effect of colorful informality was considered particularly suitable for bedrooms. Pictured left of the Uihlein mantel is an earthenware tile of tulips arranged in a geometric pattern made about 1909 by the Mueller Mosaic Tile Company, Trenton, New Jersey.

A sampling of the astonishing variety of American tiles made between 1880 and 1910 is shown on this page, clockwise from upper left: a group of eight tiles made by the J. and J. G. Low Art Tile Works, Chelsea, Massachusetts (1879-1902); a group of eleven tiles made by the Cambridge Art Tile Works, Covington, Kentucky (1887-89); a group of six tiles made by the Grueby Faience and Tile Company, Boston, Massachusetts (1895-1910); and a stoneware tile in a geometric pattern made about 1900 by the Providential Tile Works, Trenton, New Jersey.

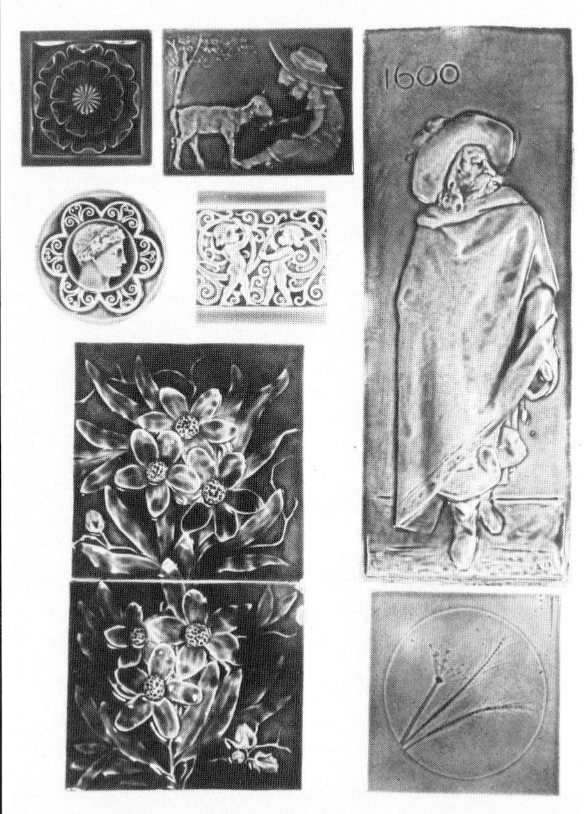

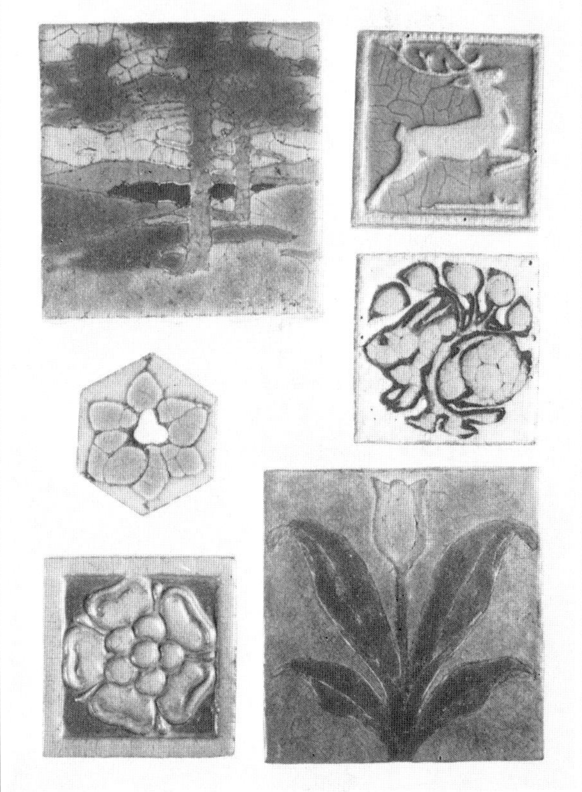

FABRICS

Opposite page: Many of the most striking textile designs of the mid- and late nineteenth century derive from Renaissance ecclesiastical fabrics in only a few colors and gold outlining. This elegant green and gold diapered design was borrowed from a German altar hanging in the 1870s and was reworked as a pattern for wool carpeting.

Of all materials used in Victorian decorating, fabrics are by far the most appealing and seductive to the eye and touch. How easy it is to linger amid the samples of soft silk brocades, crinkly cotton chintzes, and plush velvets which are displayed in the fabric showroom. And how difficult to choose between the colorful patterns—intricate paisleys and smart plaids, finely-figured geometric designs, and florals bursting with summertime freshness.

Textiles have dozens of uses in an imaginative Victorian setting, for curtains, drapes, valances and lambrequins, floor coverings, upholstery, pillows and cushions, bed hangings, and throws, to list only the most obvious. Because the commercial production of textiles increased so dramatically throughout the 1800s, it was possible for the Victorian housewife to indulge her desire for large and small decorative effects. And so it is again today by making effective use of a wide range of well-documented woven and printed reproductions. While one may have to compromise on the type of fabric chosen, synthetic blends being less expensive than 100% natural fibers, there need be no lessening of form or style.

For many years high-quality fabric manufacturers have copied nineteenth-century textiles. Since most fabrics age rather rapidly, it is necessary to replace them from time to time lest a room become, like Miss Favisham's parlor, a melancholy study in tatters. Only carpets appear to fade with beauty. A small supply of antique fabrics is always available, but at high prices; the better alternative is to draw on the well-documented designs of American and European manufacturers or even to use adaptations of these. The Victorians were never reluctant to mix and match, and neither should be today's tasteful decorator.

A Draper's Paradise

The proper draping of windows, doors, and countless objects throughout the Victorian house was the subject of many articles in contemporary women's magazines. The effects obtained from the use of fabrics, whether arranged by a professional draper or the housewife, ranged from the sublime to the downright fussy. By the 1860s the practice of decorating windows with lace or muslin undercurtains and heavy drawn-back drapes of such materials as damask, velvet, and chintz was well established; drapes were also hung in doorways as portières. The types of fabrics and patterns commonly used are readily available today and add stylish character to any period interior.

The Victorians are often criticized for excessive draping, stuffing, and padding. Until at least the 1860s, however, the use of fabric was reasonably restrained. In the Patrick Barry House, Rochester, New York (1855-57), the double parlor *(above)* is simply but stylishly decorated with heavy draperies at the window. The gracefully-drawn fabric and lace undercurtains fall behind a neo-Grec cornice and fringed valance similar to the 1853 design at the right. Two sets of portière curtains of the same type *(left)* divide the two parlors.

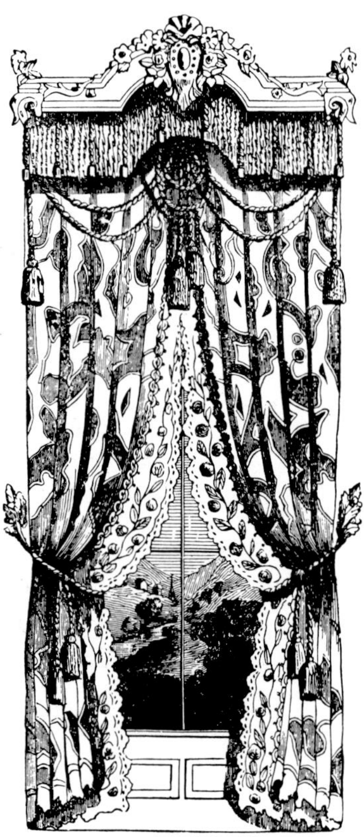

In the late 1800s a passion for grand French and Italian decorative effects of the 17th and 18th centuries, including the use of tapestries, swept into vogue in urban circles. Dr. William Richardson's Boston parlor was theatrically transformed in the 1890s with the hanging of matching pastoral scenes in a windowed alcove.

The dignified Renaissance Revival interiors of the Park-McCullough House, North Bennington, Vermont, have been treated with special care over the years. Built in 1865-66, the house is now a museum. One corner of the library *(opposite page)* illustrates the richness of the architectural cabinetwork found in the formal first-floor rooms. The ornately-patterned draperies, the design of which dates from later in the century, are simply hung on a rod. At the window are only interior shutters to filter light and to provide privacy at night. Since the house was a summer residence, there is no elaborate layering of undercurtains nor an overlay of cornice or lambrequin.

The portière serves as an elegant screen with a double purpose—to soften the architectural outlines of the doorway with a touch of color and to cut down on drafts in the spacious house.

Molly Brown's town house in Denver, Colorado *(left)*, is more fancifully decorated. The home of the international silver millionairess, and unsinkable survivor of the *Titanic* disaster, took five years to build—from 1887 to 1892. As furnished now by Historic Denver, the house is a showcase of late-nineteenth-century objects. A delicate lace curtain screens the front door for privacy without sacrificing light. Sliding doors lead into a front room, and over the entryway is a gracefully-looped festoon in a period damask reproduced by Scalamandré.

Fabric Exuberance

The delightful multicolored and patterned effects achieved in Victorian draperies, wall hangings, throws, and upholstery put to shame the timid decorating schemes of the "modern" age. The Victorians were not afraid to mix and match and did not always follow the dictates of fashion arbiters who continually advised their readers through the pages of the ladies' magazines. Many of today's approved reproduction patterns and coordinated fabrics are inviting choices, but these should not

restrict the imagination. A cozy Turkish corner in warm, inviting colors and patterns becomes what you make of it; a fringed runner of silk or damask softens and enhances the lines and finish of a heavy piece of furniture such as a bureau, piano, or sideboard; fabric panels give walls a luxurious, textured look.

Opposite page, left: A floral print hung from the cornice to the floor in a bedroom corner can imaginatively define the sleeping area. Most beds, modern or antique, no longer make use of hangings and profit from being set against a fabric background. The effect, while not historically accurate, is certainly in the Victorian spirit. *Opposite page, right:* The exuberance of the Victorian decorator is enchantingly captured in the tower room of an 1890s Boston residence. *Above:* A Turkish corner, a decorating conceit popular in the late 1800s, was popular with aesthetically-inclined young adults. It has been reproduced here with eight different patterns, all from Schumacher's Victorian Collection.

Bed Hangings

Gracefully-draped bed hangings have always been an attractive amenity in a bedroom. They suggest comfort and privacy, and, as our Colonial ancestors knew, such draperies made the bed a much warmer place in winter. The Victorians, by mid-century the beneficiaries of increasingly modern heating methods, gradually cut down on the amount of fabric used and often preferred half-testers from which to drape the material. The fourposter, however, continued in use with full canopy and side curtains and enjoyed renewed popularity during the Colonial Revival period of the 1890s and turn of the century.

The types of beds and bed hangings found in Victorian homes vary greatly from time to time and place to place. An early fourposter with hangings in the shape of lambrequins is used in a bedroom at Fountain Elms, Utica, New York *(above, right)*. The bed in this 1850s mansion could have been fitted as well with old-fashioned head, side, and foot curtains as this fashion persisted well into the nineteenth century. By contrast, a bedroom of the 1859 Morse-Libby House *(above, left)* is furnished with a contemporary Renaissance Revival bed with half-tester. It is cosseted in a fringed silk lambrequin, lace side curtains, and a tufted back panel. The twin brass beds in one of the principal bedrooms of the 1865-66 Park-McCullough House, Bennington, Vermont *(opposite page)*, also have half-testers. These are draped with muslin for summer use.

Lambrequins and Lace

The correct formula for decorating windows in the formal rooms of a mid- to late-Victorian home included the use of lambrequins, drapes, and undercurtains or shades of some sort. Like a valance, a lambrequin is an architectural ornament, and, while often of singular aesthetic appeal, its practical purpose was to hide the window casing and the apparatus used for hanging the drapes and curtains. Lace, available in infinite varieties, softened the glare of daylight and imparted a pleasant patterning to the windows. Cloth shades or wood shutters might be used along with the curtaining or in its place.

Lambrequins are made in fabrics of almost every sort, with heavier solid-color weights often chosen for their tailored appearance. As illustrated in the Morse-Libby House parlor *(opposite page, above)*, the material is hung quite tightly. A cutout scalloped shape is the standard form, and this is embellished with fringe and tassels hung either with the fringe, as in the photograph of an 1890s parlor *(opposite page, below)*, or draped across and down the sides.

Lace curtains are among the most delightful of Victorian furnishings. Shades were often conveniently used in their place, but the effect is less pleasing. The lace curtains used in a parlor window of San Francisco Plantation, Reserve, Louisiana *(above, left)* could not be improved upon. In the 1890s, such fine material could even be purchased from Montgomery, Ward *(above, right)*. Lace of this type is still available from American and European suppliers, the two examples shown at left being representative of today's lacemaking art.

Rugs and Carpets

Contrary to popular belief, floors in most Victorian houses were not smothered by wall-to-wall carpeting, whether of a floral or more austere pattern. Since broad carpeting had yet to be introduced, it was necessary to lay down narrow strips side-by-side, a procedure requiring great skill. The areas most frequently carpeted in this manner were the parlor, dining room, and the master bedroom. Other rooms, nevertheless, were not without some type of decorative overlay. Square floral or geometric-patterned carpets, floorcloths of an oilcloth substance (the precursor of linoleum), runners, and rag rugs were strategically placed for maximum effect and usefulness. Luxurious Oriental carpets were found in the homes of the wealthy throughout the century.

A floor covering for a bedroom might be nothing more than a floral carpet square placed in the center of the room, as it is in the Park-McCullough House, North Bennington, Vermont *(opposite page)*. A residence used primarily during the summer months, it was furnished more lightly than a year-round home. Bare floors at least appeared cooler, and, when left largely free of floor coverings, were easier to clean. Seen clockwise from the upper right are other types of period floor coverings; "The Oaks," a 27-inch Brussels weave reproduced by Scalamandré from a carpet in the home of Booker T. Washington in Tuskegee, Alabama; an 1851 floorcloth design; a 27-inch custom-made Wilton-weave reproduction by Langhorne Carpet; and "Waterford," a 27-inch Brussels weave based on a pattern found in the home of Sir John MacDonald, Canada's first prime minister, and reproduced by Scalamandré.

The opportunities for decorating with various materials, colors, and patterns were almost endless for the inventive Victorian. When funds were not sufficient to employ the skill of an upholsterer or draper, homemade copies could be stitched by machine or hand. All of the popular ladies' magazines supplied a continuous flow of suggestions and practical patterns. Even designs for such lowly articles as antimacassars or tidies were supplied to keep the housewife happy and occupied: "A fresh pretty tidy, either white or in colors, agreeing with or harmonizing the prevailing colors of the room, should adorn both the room, and also the mistress of the household herself," wrote one breathlessly enthusiastic Victorian tastemaker.

Fifteen different textiles can be seen in the photograph of one end of an 1890s parlor *(opposite page)*. The materials are used in both homemade and professionally-wrought objects—furniture upholstery, cushions, carpeting, drapes, curtains, throws, wall hangings, hearth rug, lamp shade, table cloth, and mantel lambrequin. The crowning achievement is surely the pieced crazy-quilt mantel lambrequin.

Only by contrast is the mid-century library of an Alexandria, Virginia, town house *(left)* a study in sobriety. Solid-color silk and velvet are used for the upholstery, and draped on the mantel is "Kerchief Stripe," a Schumacher reproduction of a Victorian fabric.

The Great Cover-Up

If it were possible to travel back in time, it would be fun to ask questions of the Victorian decorator —both professional and amateur—on the whys and wherefores of fashions in furnishings. Presented with pictorial evidence, many a decorator would confess to a madness for draping. Chairs, mantels, easels, windows, doors, tables, pianos—almost every object and architectural element was a candidate for embellishment with fabrics. Just as Whistler's mother would not look right without a shawl, the Victorian parlor of the second half of the nineteenth century doesn't appear finished without added fabric touches.

Making a Choice

The preservation movement has fostered the manufacture of reproduction fabrics, many true documentary designs and others adapatations worthy of careful consideration. Fortunately, unless one's home is to be treated as a museum, there is no one "correct" pattern. Rather, there are numerous designs appropriate for any period of the 1800s to choose from. Although one color combination may be the documented source on which the reproduction is based, other combinations are usually offered as well. Economy will dictate to a large extent the type of material chosen.

Among the most appealing nineteenth-century patterns are those created by William Morris and reproduced by a number of firms. Morris's multicolor designs of the 1880s, "Strawberry Thief" and "Loddon" *(below* and *above, right)*, are handprinted by Scalamandré on 100% cotton. Earlier in the century paisley designs, favored by Queen Victoria, were enormously popular. "Paisley Tapestry" *(below, right)* in royal blue is included in Schumacher's Victorian Collection. On the opposite page is a Renaissance Revival design of the 1850s of appropriate richness.

Decorating with Flowers

Exuberant floral designs are to be found in almost as many varieties as those possessed by nature itself. Reproduction glazed chintzes with a crisp finish and well-defined patterns are especially attractive choices for early- to mid-Victorian rooms. A majority of the designs originated in England or France, a cachet which made them even more desirable in the eyes of the American housewife. The importation of such fabrics eventually led to their imitation by nineteenth-century American manufacturers.

"Roses and Ribbons," a glazed chintz from Brunschwig & Fils *(below, left)* is an original American design well-suited for a Rococo Revival parlor. "Charleston Iris" *(below, right)*, from Scalamandré, is an earlier Victorian pattern more at home in a neo-classical setting. On the opposite page *(above, left)* is a strong geometric design, "Napoleon III," c. 1870-90. The clusters of pink and white peonies are reproduced by Brunschwig & Fils against either a green or slate-blue background. At the upper right is another French design, "Deneuve," available from Schumacher. "Pillar" *(below, left)* is an English design dated c. 1815-30, but appropriate for an early formal Victorian parlor. "Victorian Garden" *(below, right)* is a very fanciful design in glazed chintz from Brunschwig & Fils and is dated c. 1850.

Summer

10

ADDED TOUCHES

Opposite page: A treasure trove of Victoriana, small mementoes of the past which bring the past dramatically alive.

So much of what we consider indubitably Victorian today are the fine objects which once appeared to occupy nearly every corner of an overstuffed parlor—slender porcelain vases, keepsakes and mementoes of metal and glass, intricately carved wood stands and picture frames, a glimmering tea set with a delicate Oriental design, and fragile china cups and saucers. Mere clutter? We thought so not so very long ago. But, then, anything Victorian was once considered hopelessly passé. The attic seemed the only appropriate place for such antique knick-knacks. There are few such attics left unexplored today. Back to the parlor has come the intricately-carved étagère and its display of figurines and other small treasures. Proudly ensconced once more on the mantel is the resonant wood-cased parlor clock, its steady tick-tock a welcome relief from the nasty buzz of a digital timepiece. And elsewhere throughout the house are welcome reminders of the inventiveness and craftsmanship of Victorian artisans: a lovely china-head doll decorates the playroom, along with brightly colored tin and wood toys; entertaining and charming examples of lithographed sheet music are displayed on the piano; picturesque prints and early photographs, rendered more appealing by age, hang in the dining room and bedroom. There is hardly a room in the house which is not made more inviting by the addition of these and a multitude of other colorful objects.

The Image of an Age

There's one element of Victorian clutter that's well worth emulating today—and that's the banking of groups of period photographs in a variety of ornamental frames on fireplace mantels and side tables. The earliest photographs—Daguerreotypes and Ambrotypes—came in their own ornamental cases and are rare collector's items. But the introduction of the glass-plate Collodion process in mid-century, and the ensuing popularity of the *carte-de-visite*, brought photographic portraits into virtually every parlor in America. These images, torn from the plush albums and handsome frames that once contained them, can be found at bargain prices in flea markets from coast to coast. The person who doesn't have ancestral photos of his own should buy them up, frame them appropriately, and create a Victorian "family" to be proud of and display.

The variety of Victorian frames is almost endless. The examples shown here and on the facing page include two cast-iron stands, a magnificent porcelain wall frame, a pair of matching carved-wood ovals, a homemade crisscross frame, a handcrafted beaded oval, and a miniature rustic easel made from evergreen twigs.

Because our forebears posed for their unsmiling photographs with stiff and upright postures, any decorative massing of grim-faced portraits can be saved from Victorian "high seriousness" by the inclusion of photographs of children and of popular entertainers of the day. Included here among portraits of the Deats family of Pittstown, New Jersey, are photographs of actress Julia Marlowe and the low-comedy Knight Brothers.

"Try These Over On Your Piano"

The nineteenth century, like the Renaissance it so loved to imitate, was an age of music. Since any young woman of character was expected to excel not only in needlework but in such polite cultural pursuits as drawing and musical performance, evenings spent around the pianoforte or parlor organ were common family entertainments. Until Edison's phonograph, which Ambrose Bierce defined as "an irritating toy that restores life to dead noises," began to diminish its influence, sheet music was the chief disseminator of popular music across the land. Transcriptions of arias from contemporary operas, airs from the scores of ballets, and sentimental ballads, comic songs, and patriotic anthems sung by the popular entertainers of the day found their way to the keyboards of American parlors in sheet music with gaily decorated covers.

Nineteenth-century sheet music, in various states of preservation, is readily available at flea markets. Because it is not as colorful nor as popular as music from the 1920s and '30s, late-Victorian sheet music is generally found at the bottom of the pile, dog-eared, unloved, and underpriced. Buy it. Like the samples on these pages, it will dress up a piano in a Victorian parlor as no piano shawl can.

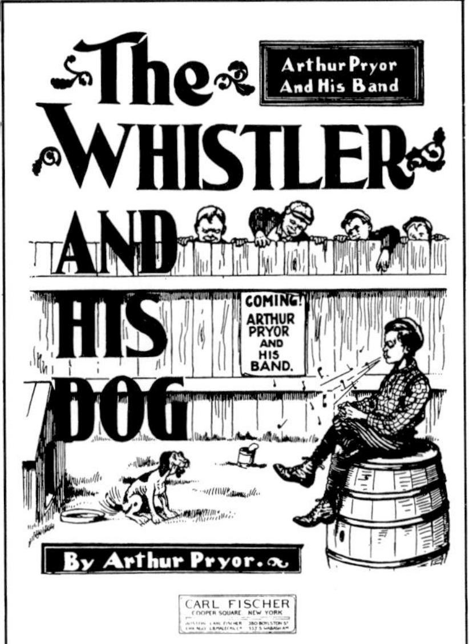
The Whistler and His Dog
Arthur Pryor And His Band
COMING! ARTHUR PRYOR AND HIS BAND.
By Arthur Pryor.
CARL FISCHER

THE LATEST CRAZE.
LITTLE ANNIE ROONEY.
SONG AND CHORUS.
WRITTEN, COMPOSED AND SUNG BY
MICHAEL NOLAN.
40
HITCHCOCK'S MUSIC STORES

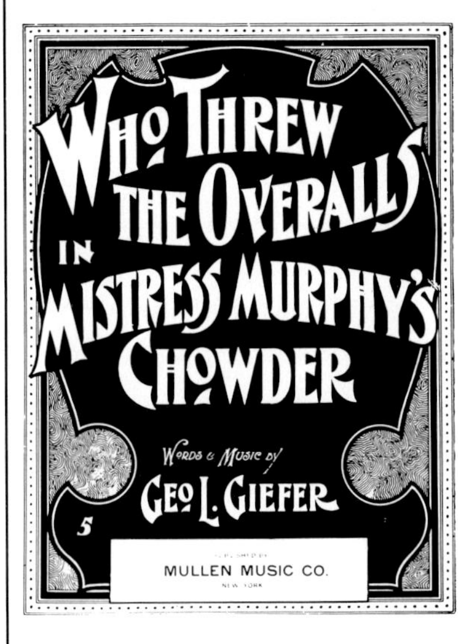
Who Threw the Overalls in Mistress Murphy's Chowder
Words & Music by
Geo L. Giefer
5
MULLEN MUSIC CO.

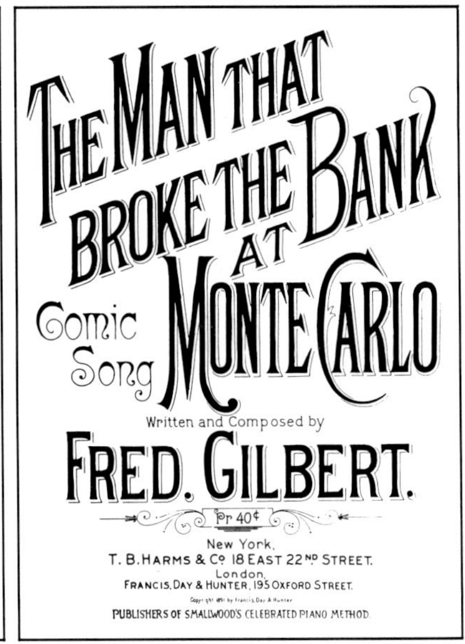
The Man that Broke the Bank at Monte Carlo
Comic Song
Written and Composed by
FRED. GILBERT.
Pr 40¢
New York,
T. B. HARMS & Co 18 EAST 22ND STREET.
London,
FRANCIS, DAY & HUNTER, 195 OXFORD STREET.
PUBLISHERS OF SMALLWOOD'S CELEBRATED PIANO METHOD

JOSEPH J. SULLIVAN'S
Celebrated
COMIC SONG
Where Did You Get That Hat?
NEW-YORK
HARDING'S MUSIC OFFICE
FOR SALE AT ALL MUSIC STORES

DEDICATED TO THE
New York Sunday World.
The Band Played On
WORDS BY
JOHN F. PALMER.
MUSIC BY
Chas. B. Ward.
THE NEW-YORK MUSIC CO

I Don't Want to
Play in Your Yard
WORDS BY
PHILIP WINGATE
4
MUSIC BY
H. W. PETRIE
PUBLISHED BY
PETRIE MUSIC COMPANY,
4627 Champlain Avenue,
CHICAGO, ILL

A First Night Hit.
Introduced & Sung with Phenomenal Success by
"The Little Magnet" - Lottie Gilson.
"Mother was a Lady"
or
"If Jack Were Only Here".
Beautiful Ballad.
Words by
Edw. B. Marks
Author of
Music by
Jos. W. Stern
Composer of
"The Lost Child"
"The Teacher & The Boy"
"His Last Thoughts Were of You"
"No One Ever Loved You More Than I"
and Many Other Successes.
5
Published by JOS. W. STERN & Co.

1508
LOVE'S OLD SWEET SONG.
WORDS BY
G. CLIFTON BINGHAM.
MUSIC BY
J. L. MOLLOY.
Price, 35 Cents.
NEW YORK:
PUBLISHED BY
RICHARD A. SAALFIELD,
41 UNION SQUARE,

THE ORIGINAL CREATION
Ta! Ra! Ra! Boom De Ay!
As Sung by
Miss Lottie Collins
in
Miss Helyett.
BROMO-SELTZER CURES
all HEADACHES and NEURALGIA
TRIAL BOTTLES 10¢ SOLD EVERYWHERE

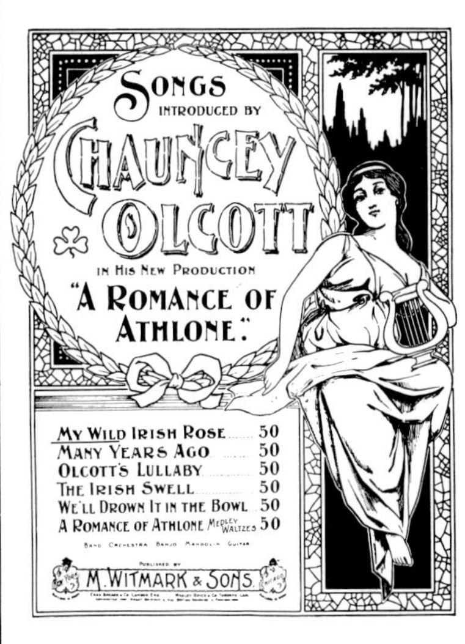
Songs
Introduced by
Chauncey Olcott
in His New Production
"A Romance of Athlone."
My Wild Irish Rose 50
Many Years Ago 50
Olcott's Lullaby 50
The Irish Swell 50
We'll Drown It in the Bowl 50
A Romance of Athlone Medley Waltzes 50
M. WITMARK & SONS

The Song that Beats "McGinty."
"THE CAT CAME BACK"
WORDS AND MUSIC BY
HARRY S. MILLER,
AUTHOR OF
4
PUBLISHED BY
WILL ROSSITER,
THE POPULAR SONG PUBLISHER,
MAIN OFFICES, 56 FIFTH AVE., CHICAGO.

The World in Miniature

Scratch a man and you'll find the boy beneath the skin. Long before the current craze for Victoriana placed a hefty price tag on virtually everything from the period, grown men discovered a nostalgic world that could be re-created from nineteenth-century toys. So avidly have Victorian toys been collected that the very best examples are well beyond the pocketbooks of most. Still, the desire to unhook the miniature ladders from a cast-iron fire engine or to pull the cow-catchered engine of a tin train is strong indeed. So the search goes on. Like Citizen Kane's sled, "Rosebud," nineteenth-century toys continue to cast their powerful spell. Fortunately, pieces *can* be found in antique shops and at auctions, and, for

Above (top): Clowns on a rotating seesaw, a tin clockwork toy imported from Germany, (c. 1895). *Above:* "ABC Nine-Pin and Spelling Blocks," an educational toy, manufactured by McLoughlin Brothers of New York in 1887, that claimed to help Johnny to spell, if not to bowl. *Right:* An 1879 advertisement that hails building blocks as "among the most pleasing and instructive toys ever invented for boys and girls."

Above (top): A boy in a silk cap and jacket riding a velocipede, an iron automaton made by Ives, Blakeslee and Co. of Bridgeport, Connecticut, in the 1870s. When the clockwork mechanism is wound, the velocipede moves and the boy's hands wave back and forth. *Above:* A cast-iron hoop toy from the same period by George W. Brown and Co. of Forestville, Connecticut. When the mechanism is wound, the hoop runs in circles.

those whose sense of whimsy is greater than their purses, there is a vast array of reproductions. Antique toys were originally meant to instill manly virtues in little boys. Today, appropriately displayed in Victorian settings, they can help make little boys of men.

Clockwise from upper left: A tin fire engine by George W. Brown (1860); the "Electra," a tin steamboat from the same period by the same maker; a cast-iron hook and ladder by the Wilkins Toy Co. of Keene, New Hampshire (1895); the "Lyon" locomotive with mail and passenger cars, a tin train set by an unknown maker (1870); and a group of "Nodders"—caricatures that nod their heads (1890s).

Playthings for "Little Mothers"

Victorian moralists rationalized their children's love of dolls by inventing high-minded reasons for such natural inclinations. Little girls, who were expected to dress their dolls in the latest Parisian styles, could both practice the art of needlework and develop the "good taste" required to observe the elaborate etiquette of high-Victorian fashion. Moreover, by playing with baby dolls, they were expected to develop the "tender sensibilities" needed for future motherhood. The "little mothers," however, knew better. To them, dolls were just plain fun.

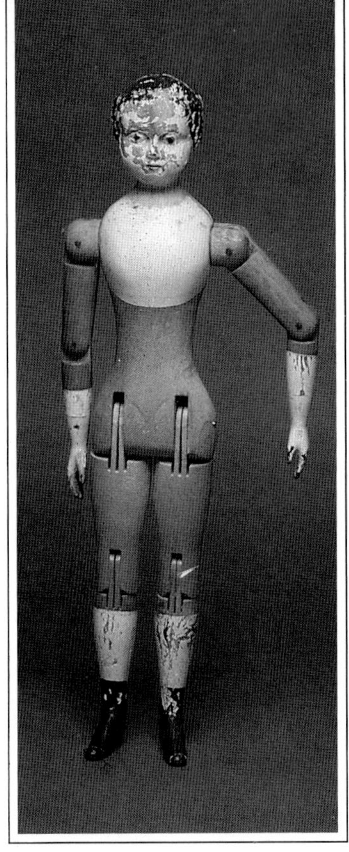

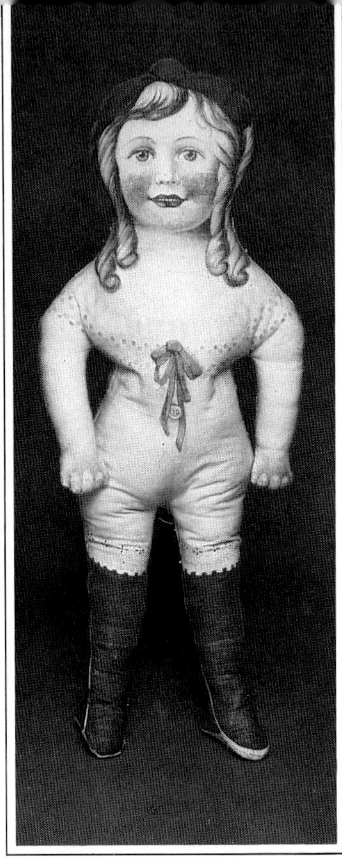

Left: "The Dolls' Tea Party," an engraving in *Harper's Bazar* (1872), illustrates the Victorian ideal: little girls perfect needlework skills and keep abreast of high fashion by dressing French lady dolls, and practice for future motherhood by nurturing baby dolls. *Above:* A wooden doll with mortise-and-tenon joints designed by Joel Ellis for the Co-operative Mfg. Co. of Springfield, Vermont (1873), and a lithographed rag doll produced by the Art Fabric Mills of New York City (1900). *Opposite page (clockwise from upper left):* china dolls, made from parts imported from Germany, assembled in American toy stores, and dressed by their new owners; a French bisque lady doll by Maison Huret (c. 1880); Thomas Alva Edison's phonograph doll (c. 1890) produced by Maison Jumeau in Paris and sold in the United States by Edison himself; a topsy-turvy doll suggested by the characters of Topsy and Eva in *Uncle Tom's Cabin;* and a papier-mâché doll imported from Germany (c. 1870).

Unquestionably the golden age of dolls, the nineteenth century witnessed the production of every conceivable type, from humble rag doll to exquisite French bisque. With doll-collecting now the nation's number-one hobby, no Victorian home should be without a nursery of nineteenth-century dolls, either authentic or reproduction, or both. Little girls still love dolls. And so do their mothers.

The Stone Ideal

America's sculptors of the Victorian era sought to celebrate the people's heroes and favorite characters, whether out of Shakespeare or the Revolutionary tradition. In technique they imitated the work of European artists, and often followed the neo-classical dictates of Rome. Marble, however, was not the usual medium. Parian was much more common in the mid-century, and as the production of this chalky white porcelain was improved, statues, statuettes, figurines, and sculptured vases were widely available to the public. The skill of the Victorian modelers varied greatly, but the charm of their work is incontestable. If one could not possess a heroic bust or monumental sculpture, there were always small figures—of animals and birds—and statuettes of entwined lovers or sportsmen in action. Later in the century, bronze figures, holding aloft a light in Statue of Liberty style, achieved great popularity in the home. The Victorians loved the concept of the ideal, of virtue and beauty, and they sought it in their sculpture in every way.

Love of the works of the Bard was celebrated in sculpture by popular artist John Rogers in the 1880s. The scene from *Othello (above)* was one of the classier compositions of this early Norman Rockwell. The graceful use to which Parian could be put is shown in *The Tight Shoe* (c. 1850), a sweetly sentimental figure *(right)* created by the U.S. Pottery Co. of Bennington, Vermont. *Opposite page:* The Trenton firm of Ott & Brewer produced excellent Parian busts, one of them Isaac Broome's *Benjamin Franklin* (1876). The "Gloria Ball Swing" (c. 1900) is a bronze sculpture, nearly three-feet high, that, with its swinging pendulum, functions as a clock. Truly monumental sculpture, however, found its rightful place in the homes of America's industrial tycoons, in this case Lyndhurst, the Tarrytown, New York, estate of Jay Gould.

FRANKLIN

Floral Elegancies

Passion for the beauty of nature swept away even the modest, home-bound Victorian housewife on a tide of do-it-yourself horticulture. Poetic landscapes on the wall, stuffed birds, pressed flowers, and pot-pourri would not suffice. Sticks were fashioned into "rustic work"; ivy was draped from cornices and mantels; fuschias and ferns swung from brackets; palms and other exotic species decorated the parlor and dining room. One needn't have a conservatory in order to simulate a hothouse atmosphere. There is little here that anyone would want to emulate today. Our love of natural composition runs counter to the Victorian impulse to contrive every possible floral artifice. Many of the containers they used, however—vases in porcelain, pottery, and glass—will find a welcome home in our own sunny bowers. Some of those illustrated here are so beautiful that they probably stood alone without floral tribute, and such might be their use today, as stunning decorative accents.

The Victorians were the original do-it-yourself florists, appropriating every possible type of plant (and animal) life to embellish their interiors.

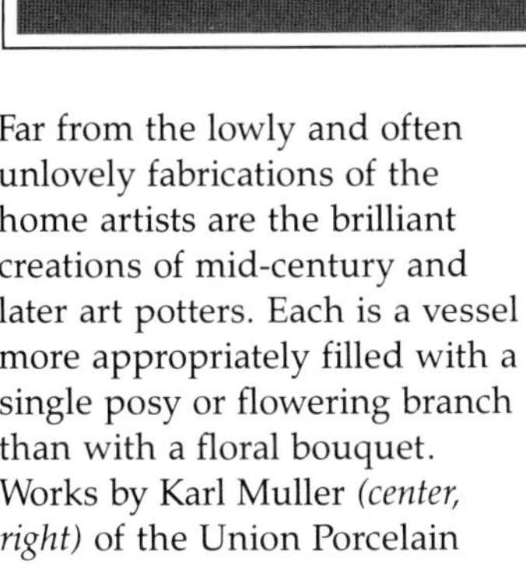

Far from the lowly and often unlovely fabrications of the home artists are the brilliant creations of mid-century and later art potters. Each is a vessel more appropriately filled with a single posy or flowering branch than with a floral bouquet. Works by Karl Muller *(center, right)* of the Union Porcelain Works are American classics, as are pieces from the Matt Morgan Art Pottery of Cincinnati *(bottom)* and the elaborate grape-strewn Parian vase from the U.S. Pottery Co. of Bennington, Vermont *(above)*. Imitations of handcrafted art pottery were widely produced for general use and may be easily found today.

The Victorian Table: Silver

Fine silver objects for the table were the dream of every Victorian housewife, and, by the end of the century, these wares—in sterling or silver plate—had found a handsome niche in many a corner cupboard or serving table. Rogers Bros. and competing manufacturers throughout the Northeast mastered the old silversmith's art and advertised their wares in everything from magazines to mail-order catalogues. Bells, chafing dishes, platters, pitchers, tea and coffee sets, bonbon dishes, napkin rings, and, of course, flatware, flowed in amazing variety and abundance from the factories. Much of this ware is highly decorative, with applied, répoussé, or engraved touches that make of the simplest object something of aesthetic uniqueness. Even lowly Brittania metal and other plated pieces have a form pleasing to the eye. All types of Victorian silver are to be found today in antique shops and flea markets, their value only increasing with time.

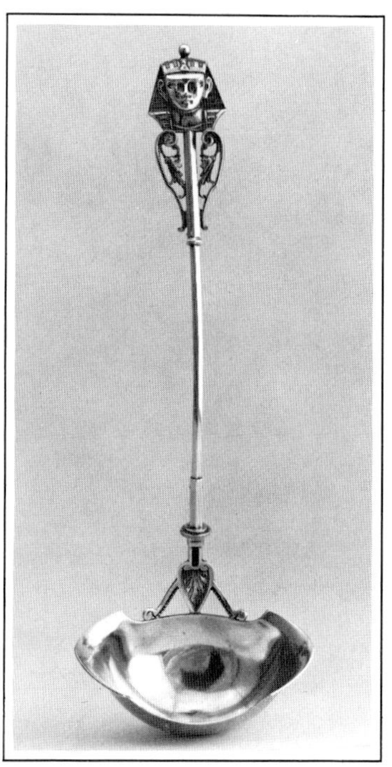

The table is set for dinner at the James Whitcomb Riley House in Indianapolis, Indiana. A porcelain soup tureen, soup bowls, and silver flatware rest on a lace tablecloth. Silver serving pieces, displayed on the sideboard, are ready for use. The sterling dinner bell *(right)* was made by the Gorham Mfg. Co. in 1884; the Pharaonic punch ladle, by Wood & Hughes in 1865.

Clockwise from upper left: silver-plated tilting pitcher for ice water by the Pairpoint Mfg. Co. (1885); sterling centerpiece by Tiffany & Co. (c. 1872); sterling smoking set (tray, cigarette urns, and ashtray) by Wm. B. Kerr & Co. (c. 1900); turn-of-the-century napkin rings by unknown makers and marked "Don," "Fred," and "Carrie"; sterling-plated coffee urn by John Carrow (c. 1885); silver-plated pickle caster with pressed-glass jar and plated pickle tongs by Barbour Silver Co. (c. 1890); sterling ewer, designed by George B. Sharp for Bailey & Co. (c. 1848).

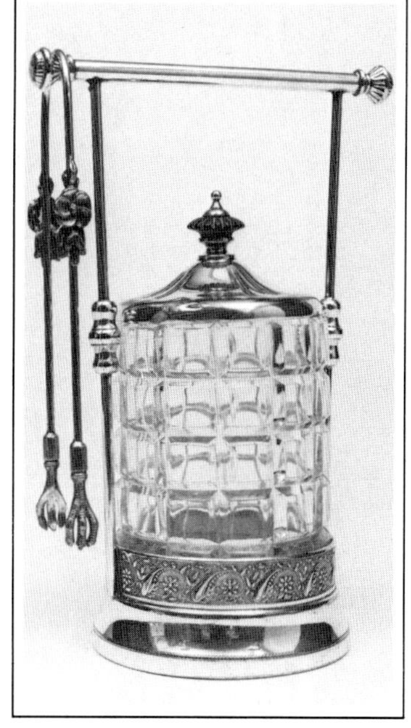

The Victorian Table: Glass and Porcelain

Among the most beautiful and useful of decorative Victorian objects are those produced in extraordinary profusion by glassmakers and potters. There was a glass container for just about everything—lemonade, punch, berries, candy, condiments, celery, syrup, cream, salt—and enormous sets of glass dishes were commonplace. It is remarkable that so many of the objects, produced in an almost assembly-line fashion, are so artfully formed and decorated. The potters were equally skilled in producing attractive table and kitchenware that could last for generations.

Below: A pressed-glass decanter in the "Pillar and Bull's-Eye" pattern with a pewter stopper, probably by Bakewell, Pears & Co. (c. 1850) and a pressed-glass sugar bowl in the "Sweetheart" pattern by the Boston and Sandwich Glass Co. (c. 1845). *Right, top row:* a cranberry pressed-glass pitcher in the "Thumbprint" pattern (c. 1880) and an art glass cruet (c. 1880); *center row:* a milk-glass compote in the "Grape" pattern (c. 1900) and a frosted pressed-glass covered dish in the form of a hen (c. 1880); *bottom row:* a brilliant cut-glass water bottle (c. 1900) and a pressed-glass sauce dish in the "Horn of Plenty" pattern by the Boston and Sandwich Glass Co. (c. 1850).

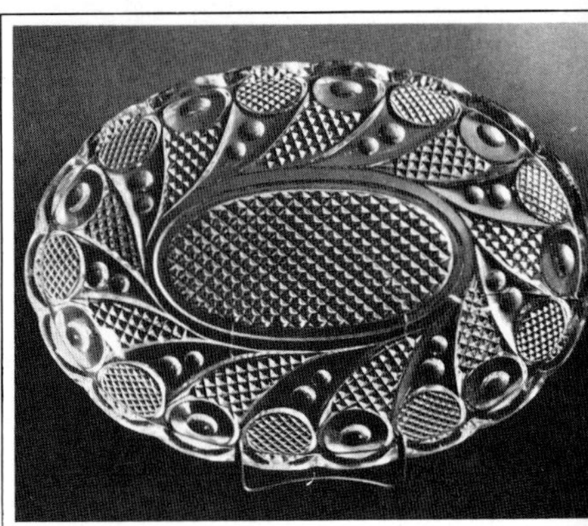

Clockwise from upper left: a molded belleek tea set by Morris and Willmore (c. 1895); a hand-decorated artificial porcelain cake plate by Kurlbaum and Schwartz (c. 1853); an engraved silvered-glass bowl (c. 1880); a hand-decorated porcelain dish in the shape of a leaf by the Ceramic Art Co. (c. 1890); a cup and saucer decorated with flowers and framed with gold by Charles Cartlidge & Co. (c. 1850).

Tempus Fugit

The nineteenth century witnessed the emergence of America as the principal clockmaker of the world. Applying the principles of mass production to the young clock industry of New England, American inventiveness succeeded in the gradual miniaturization of timekeepers from the handsome, but bulky, grandfather clock of the previous century to small, portable cabinets that could sit comfortably on a table or a mantel. It succeeded as well in reducing the price of a clock so that anyone who had a single dollar could afford an American timepiece. As a result, the clocks of Chauncey Jerome, Seth Thomas, Joseph Ives, Elias Ingraham, Eli Terry, and a score of other American manufacturers became household commonplaces around the world.

Although the Colonial Revival brought about a sentimental renewal of interest in the grandfather clock, the Victorian hand is most apparent in the century's innovative shelf clocks. As the photographs on the following pages show, the term "Victorian mantel clock" is almost meaningless. There are at least two dozen clearly defined (and named) categories of the type. And within each type, variety was surely the keystone of the era. In one year alone (1891) the Ansonia Clock Company offered timepieces set within bronze locomotives, sailing ships, racing trotters, peacocks, horseshoes, padlocks, and suits of armor, just to name a few. No Victorian setting should be without the steady ticking of a nineteenth-century clock.

1

2

3

Opposite page (left): Two examples of the many styles of Victorian wall clocks: a figure eight clock ("Ionic" model) by E. Ingraham & Co. (c. 1880) and a banjo timepiece by E. Howard & Co. (1860). *Opposite page (right):* A turn-of-the-century grandfather clock in the Colonial Revival style by the Waltham Clock Co. (c. 1899).

4

5

6

7

8

9

Left: Just a few of the many types of nineteenth-century shelf clocks that render obsolete the descriptive term "Victorian mantel clock": **1.** a beehive timepiece by the Waterbury Clock Co. (c. 1870); **2.** a box (or cottage) timepiece by the same manufacturer (c. 1858); **3.** a column clock by Seth Thomas (c. 1860); **4.** an ogee clock by an unknown maker (c. 1845); **5.** a steeple (or sharp Gothic) clock by Birge & Fuller (c. 1845); **6.** an acorn clock by the Forestville Mfg. Co. (c. 1845); **7.** an iron-front clock in the Gothic style by Terhune & Botsford (c. 1854); **8.** a porcelain boudoir timepiece by E. N. Welch Mfg. Co. (c. 1880); **9.** a calendar clock ("Arditi" model) by the same manufacturer (1895).

The difference between a clock and a timepiece, incidentally, is that a clock strikes the hour and a timepiece does not.

10

11

12

13

14

15

16

17

18

19

Opposite page: The inventive variety of Victorian shelf clocks is further illustrated by additional generic types, which hardly exhaust the possibilities: **10.** a "blinking eye" timepiece ("Hessian Soldier" model) by Bradley & Hubbard Mfg. Co. (c. 1857) [in such clocks the eyes move horizontally or vertically]; **11.** a round-top timepiece by the Terry Clock Co. (c. 1870); **12.** a partial-octagon clock ("Parlor Calendar No. 5" model) by Seth Thomas (c. 1875); **13.** a carriage clock (or *pendule de voyage*) by the Ansonia Clock Co. (c. 1880); **14.** a crystal regulator clock by the Boston Clock Co. (c. 1880); **15.** a figured mantel clock ("Shakespeare" model) by Ansonia (c. 1900); **16.** a cabinet (or parlor walnut) clock ("Patti" model) by E. N. Welch (1887); **17.** a kitchen (or gingerbread) clock ("Sapphire" model) by Ingraham (c. 1900); **18.** a "black" clock by Ansonia (c. 1900); **19.** a novelty timepiece by Seth Thomas (c. 1890). [The late Victorians, who occasionally give their period a bad name through the preference for high kitsch, bought novelty clocks in every conceivable and inappropriate shape.]

Right: Two steeple clocks with fine rosewood veneer cases and reverse painting on glass panels. The double steeple (or steeple-on-steeple) clock at the left is by Theodore Terry and Franklin C. Andrews (c. 1845). The sharp Gothic clock at the right is by the Ansonia Brass Co. (c. 1855).

AMERICAN VICTORIAN 

A GUIDE TO SOURCES AND SERVICES

Opposite page: With a bouquet of fresh-cut roses and Queen Anne's lace almost blending into the lushly-patterned wallpaper, a rosewood sideboard is laden with antique serving pieces and the sweetmeats of a modern Victorian feast.

A GUIDE TO SOURCES AND SERVICES

Renewed interest in Victorian decoration and architecture has led to the creation of new markets in antique and reproduction building supplies, hardware, lighting fixtures, and heating and cooking devices. When possible, of course, it is almost always preferable to purchase the old, but many reproductions are so well made today that they can blend in with the old without seeming artificial. The number of craftsmen trained to copy traditional Victorian patterns and designs increases each year, and the variety of excellent reproductions made continues to grow. This is especially true in the areas of wallcoverings and fabrics, where originals are almost impossible to come by.

The Guide to Sources and Services that follows lists suppliers of both antique and reproduction Victoriana and ranges from very large companies to individual craftsmen who can reproduce objects to your specifications. All the firms listed will respond to written or telephone inquiries about ordering their catalogues or brochures.

Omitted from this directory are sources of such accessories as those illustrated in the chapter on "Added Touches," since these and countless other nineteenth-century objects are readily available at antique shops and flea markets. Also omitted are sources of reproduction Victorian furniture. While some might disagree, we're of the opinion that such pieces have yet to reach a level of excellence where we can comfortably recommend them.

Setting the Scene

STAIRCASES

ATRA Interiors
1871 South Acoma
Denver, CO 80223
(303) 778-7545

Custom and stock stairs and stair parts.

Boston Turning Works
42 Plympton Street
Boston, MA 02118
(617) 482-9085

Architectural millwork and custom wood turning.

James Dean
62 Pioneer Street
Cooperstown, NY 13326
(607) 547-2262

A craftsman who specializes in architectural stairbuilding and handrailing.

Haas Wood & Ivory Works
64 Clementina Street
San Francisco, CA 94105
(415) 421-8273

Custom woodworking including newels, balusters, and finials.

Industrial Woodworking
1331 Leithton Road
Mundelein, IL 60060
(312) 367-9080

Custom-milled quality stair parts.

Mad River Wood Works
4935 Boyd Road, Box 163
Arcata, CA 95521
(707) 826-0629

Fine millwork items including balusters and stair parts.

Silverton Victorian Mill Works
Box 523
Silverton, CO 81433
(303) 387-5716

Stock millwork items for balusters and railings.

GLASS

Architectural Emphasis
2743 Ninth Street
Berkeley, CA 94710
(415) 644-2737

Among other glass products, this company carries full beveled-glass panels.

S. A. Bendheim Company
122 Hudson Street
New York, NY 10013
(212) 226-6370

Stained-glass materials and hand-blown glass panes.

Bevel-Rite Manufacturing Company
3434 Highway 9
Freehold, NJ 07728
(201) 462-8462

Colored mirrors and glass as well as bevels of various sizes.

Morgan Bockius Studios, Inc.
1412 Old York Road
Warminster, PA 18974
(215) 674-1930

Custom-made stained glass for doors and windows.

Sandra Brauer/Stained Glass
364-B Atlantic Avenue
Brooklyn, NY 11217
(212) 855-0656

A glass artist who both designs stained glass and can restore and repair old stained- and leaded-glass windows.

The Condon Studios
33 Richdale Avenue
Cambridge, MA 02140
(617) 661-5776

Decorative antique windows and glass lamps.

Electric Glass Company
1 East Mellen Street
Hampton, VA 23663
(804) 722-6200

Custom and stock beveled-glass panels.

Gargoyles, Ltd.
512 South Third Street
Philadelphia, PA 19147
(215) 629-1700

A wide selection of American, British, and European architectural antiques, including stained glass.

Ice Nine Glass Design
6128 Oldson Memorial Highway
Golden Valley, MN 55422
(612) 375-9669

Acid-etched glass for windows and doors.

Louisville Art Glass Studio
1110 Baxter Avenue
Louisville, KY 40204
(502) 585-5421

Clear and stained leaded-glass designs.

Manor Art Glass
20 Ridge Road
Douglaston, NY 11363
(212) 631-8029

Stained-glass repair and restoration.

Pocahontas Hardware & Glass
Box 127
Pocahontas, IL 62275
(618) 699-2880

Imaginative etched-glass panels suitable for cabinets, windows, and doors.

Pompei Stained Glass
455 High Street
West Medford, MA 02155
(617) 395-8861

Stained-glass windows and cabinet and ceiling panels.

The Rambusch Company
40 West 13th Street
New York, NY 10011
(212) 675-0400

One of the nation's leaders in stained-glass design and restoration, primarily for large-scale projects.

J. Ring Stained Glass Studio, Inc.
618 North Washington Avenue
Minneapolis, MN 55401
(612) 332-1769

Beveled-glass panels, including transoms and sidelights.

Shadovitz Brothers, Inc.
1565 Bergen Street
Brooklyn, NY 11213
(212) 774-9100

Sheet glass in various colors, as well as bent glass and glazier's tools.

Walton Stained Glass
209 Railway
Campbell, CA 95008
(408) 866-0533

A good source for imaginative beveled-glass window designs as well as stained-glass work and sandblasted mirrors.

WOODWORK

Anderson & McQuaid, Inc.
170 Fawcett Street
Cambridge, MA 02138
(617) 876-3250

Architectural millwork and moldings.

Art Directions
6120 Delmar
St. Louis, MO 63112
(314) 863-1895

Architectural antiques including carved ornaments and columns, as well as custom millwork.

Bendix Mouldings, Inc.
235 Pegasus Avenue
Northvale, NJ 07647
(201) 767-8888

Decorative wood moldings and ornamentation.

Boston Turning Works
42 Plympton Street
Boston, MA 02118
(617) 482-9085

Architectural millwork and custom wood turning.

Cumberland Woodcraft Company
2500 Walnut Bottom Road
Carlisle, PA 17013
(717) 243-0063

Made-to-order paneling and wainscoting, along with a wide range of decorative millwork.

Depot Woodworking, Inc.
683 Pine Street
Burlington, VT 05401
(802) 658-5670

This company can match existing moldings as well as provide a stock line of paneling and wainscoting.

The Emporium
2515 Morse Street
Houston, TX 77019
(713) 528-3808

Made-to-order gingerbread, fretwork, and gable trim.

Gargoyles, Ltd.
512 South Third Street
Philadelphia, PA 19147
(215) 629-1700

Architectural antiques from Britain, Europe, and America; the selection includes paneling, posts and rails, and mantels.

Haas Wood & Ivory Works
64 Clementina Street
San Francisco, CA 94105
(415) 421-8273

Custom woodwork including brackets, scrolls, and moldings.

Island City Wood Working Company
1801 Mechanic Street
Galveston, TX 77550
(713) 765-5727

Every possible type of wood trim for Victorian structures.

Chip Lapointe
186 Emerson Place
Brooklyn, NY 11205
(212) 857-8594

Handcrafted old house elements including shutters, windows, doors, mantels, and inlay work.

Mad River Wood Works
4935 Boyd Road, Box 163
Arcata, CA 95521
(707) 826-0629

Fine millwork including fence pickets, screen doors, and shingles.

Maine Architectural Millwork
Front Street
South Berwick, ME 03908
(207) 384-9541

A wide range of custom millwork and other restoration products.

Old Colony Crafts
Box 155
Liberty, ME 04949
(207) 993-2552

Detailed plans for constructing cornice moldings.

Pocahontas Hardware & Glass
Box 127
Pocahontas, IL 62275
(618) 699-2880

Solid pine doors with etched-glass panels in place.

Renovation Products
5302 Junius
Dallas, TX 75214
(214) 827-5111

Hard-to-find architectural elements, including many gable trim designs.

Rosewood Ventures
Box 610, Port Maitland,
Yarmouth County, Nova Scotia, Canada B0W 2V0
(902) 649-2782

Custom mantels, doors, wainscoting, and beams.

San Francisco Victoriana
2245 Palou Avenue
San Francisco, CA 94124
(415) 648-0313

Exhaustive selection of moldings, wainscoting, cornices, and other wood ornamentation.

Robert Seitz
Farwell Road
Tyngsboro, MA 01879
(617) 649-7707

Custom furniture and cabinetry.

Silverton Victorian Mill Works
Box 523
Silverton, CO 81433
(303) 387-5716

Wood window casings and sash molding made to order.

The Wrecking Bar of Atlanta
292 Moreland Avenue, NE
Atlanta, GA 30307
(404) 525-0468

An abundant supply of architectural antiques, including millwork, doors, and doorways.

FLOORING

Depot Woodworking, Inc.
683 Pine Street
Burlington, VT 05401
(802) 658-5670

A wide range of wood flooring, both custom and stock.

Mountain Lumber
1327 Carlton Avenue
Charlottesville, VA 22901
(804) 295-1922

Salvaged heart pine lumber remilled and available in several grades.

Tibbals Flooring Company
Oneida, TN 37841
(615) 569-8526

Oak parquet flooring which comes in kits and can be assembled by the home craftsman.

Tiresias, Inc.
Box 1864
Orangeburg, SC 29116
(803) 534-8478

Hard-to-find heart pine flooring as well as a large stock of exotic woods.

PLASTERWORK

A & M Decorative Trim & Cornices
3073 West 38th Avenue
Denver, CO 80211
(303) 477-3060

Specializes in plaster cornices, trim, and ceiling medallions.

Dovetail, Inc.
Box 1569
Lowell, MA 01853
(617) 454-2944

A complete line of moldings, ceiling designs, and medallions.

Felber Studios
110 Ardmore Avenue, Box 551
Ardmore, PA 19003
(215) 642-4710

Ornamental ceiling designs, as well as an extensive selection of plaster ceiling patterns, cornices, niches, and shells.

Focal Point, Inc.
2005 Marietta Road, NW
Atlanta, GA 30318
(404) 351-0820

Architectural ornamentation in plaster and modern polymers, specializing in ceiling cornice moldings and overdoor and window pieces.

Form & Texture
12 South Albion Street
Denver, CO 80222
(303) 388-1324

Restoration of ornamental plasterwork as well as original designs for architectural decoration.

Giannetti Studios
3806 38th Street
Brentwood, MD 20722
(301) 927-0033

Ceiling medallions and crown moldings, as well as custom designs and copies from fragments.

San Francisco Victoriana
2245 Palou Avenue
San Francisco, CA 94124
(415) 648-0313

An excellent selection of moldings, cornices, brackets, ceiling medallions, and friezes.

Horton Brasses
Nooks Hill Road, Box 95
Cromwell, CT 06416
(203) 635-4400

Plain and decorative escutcheons and matching pulls in various styles, as well as custom work.

William Hunrath Company, Inc.
153 East 57th Street
New York, NY 10022
(212) 758-0780

A good source for hard-to-find brass tubing and fasteners for stair carpeting.

Hardware

GENERAL HARDWARE

A-Ball Plumbing Supply
1703 West Burnside
Portland, OR 97209
(503) 228-0026

A good source for turn-of-the-century solid brass mechanical doorbells.

Baldwin Hardware & Manufacturing Company
841 Wyomissing Boulevard, Box 82
Reading, PA 19603
(215) 777-7811

Brass locks and latches, drop rings, knobs, and drapery and curtain hardware.

Ball & Ball
463 West Lincoln Highway
Exton, PA 19341
(215) 363-7330

An extensive selection of period door locks, hinges, pulls, knobs, and bolts.

Circecast, Inc.
380 7th Street
San Francisco, CA 94103
(415) 863-8319

Cast window catches, sash lifts, hinges, knobs, and keyholes.

Brian F. Leo
7520 Stevens Avenue South
Richfield, MN 55423
(612) 861-1473

Escutcheons, doorknobs, handles, grips, and hinges.

Period Furniture Hardware Company, Inc.
123 Charles Street
Boston, MA 02114
(617) 227-0758

Cast drawer pulls, escutchons, brass hat and coat hooks, and solid brass door knockers.

Quaker City Manufacturing Company
701 Chester Pike
Sharon Mill, PA 19079
(215) 586-4770

Sash hardware and replacement channels for old windows.

Random & Width
Box 427
West Chester, PA 19380
(215) 436-4632

Unusual designs in brass and cast-iron door knockers, as well as drapery and curtain hardware.

Renaissance Decorative Hardware
Box 332
Leonia, NJ 07605
(201) 568-1937

Hardware for sliding parlor doors, as well as hinges and pulls.

Ritter & Son Hardware
Gualala, CA 95445
(707) 884-3363 in CA
(800) 358-9120

Stamped brass keyholes, escutcheons, bin pulls, and knobs.

The Woodworkers Store
21801 Industrial Boulevard
Rogers, MN 55374
(612) 428-4101

Sockets and casters for antique furniture.

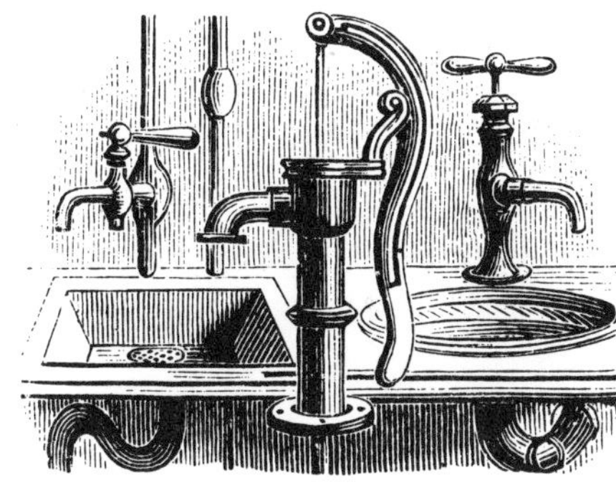

PLUMBING HARDWARE

A-Ball Plumbing Supply
1703 West Burnside
Portland, OR 97209
(503) 228-0026

Claw-foot tubs, brass and porcelain faucets, and high-tank toilets.

Fife's Woodworking & Manufacturing Company
9 Main Street
Northwood, NH 03261
(603) 942-8339

Oak and mahogany bathroom accessories.

Kohler Company
Kohler, WI 53044
(414) 457-4441

A good line of old-style sinks and tubs, as well as period-designed faucets to fit new fixtures.

P & G New & Used Plumbing Supply Company
155 Harrison Avenue
Brooklyn, NY 11205
(212) 384-6310

Claw-foot tubs and pedestal sinks as well as plumbing parts are sold in this retail shop.

Random & Width
Box 427
West Chester, PA 19380
(215) 436-4632

Lavatory and tub sets in brass or brass and porcelain.

S. Chris Rheinschild
2220 Carlton Way
Santa Barbara, CA 93109
(805) 962-8598

Unusual custom sink units in wood, copper, brass, and china.

Roy Electric Company
1054 Coney Island Avenue
Brooklyn, NY 11230
(212) 339-6311 or 761-7905

Original bathroom hardware of the period, including faucets, knobs, and tubs.

Walker Industries
Box 129
Bellevue, TX 37221
(615) 646-5084

Pedestal sinks, reproduction tubs, and custom sinks in copper and brass.

Wallcoverings

Specialty types of wallcoverings such as embossed papers, murals, and metal panels are available only from select distributors and/or manufacturers. Most papers, however, including even documentary designs or adaptations of traditional patterns, can be ordered through full-service paint and paper stores or home centers. The firms marked with an asterisk are those that deal directly with the public and will handle direct mail orders. The others listed distribute their products through retail outlets and/or interior designers. All will answer inquiries about their offerings.

*A. A. Abbingdon Ceiling Company
2149 Utica Avenue
Brooklyn, NY 11234
(212) 258-8333

A major supplier of metal ceilings and moldings.

*Laura Ashley (mail order)
Box 5308
Melville, NY 11747
(800) 523-6383

There are Ashley retail outlets throughout the United States; call the number above for the location of the shop nearest you.

A good line of Victorian-style papers in addition to the "country look" designs for which the firm is best known.

*Bassett & Vollum
217 North Main Street
Galena, IL 61036
(815) 777-2460

Extraordinary borders and wallpapers are available in hand silkscreened designs. Custom reproduction work is also undertaken.

Louis Bowen
979 Third Avenue
New York, NY 10022
(212) 392-5810

Murals, panels, and landscapes, as well as marbleized book papers and handprinted borders.

*Bradbury & Bradbury Wallpapers
Box 155
Benecia, CA 94510
(707) 746-1900

Documented wall, ceiling, and frieze papers from the late nineteenth century.

Brunschwig & Fils
979 Third Avenue
New York, NY 10022
(212) 838-7878

Documentary and adaptation papers, all expertly printed, and many suitable for nineteenth-century interiors.

*Chelsea Decorative Metal
6115 Cheena Drive
Houston, TX 77096
(713) 721-9200

Embossed metal ceilings and walls, all stamped with the original dies.

Clarence House
40 East 57th Street
New York, NY 10022
(212) 752-2890

Exclusive distributor for the documentary and adaptation papers of Cole and Son, England.

*Colefax & Fowler Designs Ltd.
39 Brook Street
London W1Y 1AU, England
(01) 439-2231

A good selection of hand-printed papers, many of which are nineteenth-century period pieces and exact reproductions. Several designs are compatible with the firm's chintzes.

Cowtan and Tout
979 Third Avenue
New York, NY 10022
(212) 753-4488

Exact reproductions of both early- and late-Victorian papers.

A. L. Diament and Company
309 Commerce Drive, Box 230
Exton, PA 19341
(215) 363-5660

French scenic papers of the late-Victorian era.

S. M. Hexter
2800 Superior Avenue
Cleveland, OH 44114
(216) 696-0146

Hexter produces and distributes the Greenfield Village patterns of the early to mid-1800's suitable for both formal and informal interiors.

Lee Jofa
979 Third Avenue
New York, NY 10022
(212) 889-3900

A small but select group of documentary English and American designs is offered.

*W. F. Norman Corporation
Box 323, 214 North Cedar Street
Nevada, MO 64772
(417) 667-5552

Original dies used in stamping out plates for ceiling centers, corners, borders, cornices, and friezes, side walls and wainscoting.

*Old Stone Mill
Adams, MA 01220
(413) 743-1015

Simple, handsomely-printed reproductions and adaptations of early- and nineteenth-century papers.

*Open Pacific Graphics
#43 Market Square
Victoria, British Columbia
Canada
(604) 388-5233

A supplier of late-Victorian designs, including William Morris papers and various other reproductions and adaptations.

*Osborne & Little Ltd.
304 Kings Road
London SW3 5UH
England

Traditional designs are attractively produced in a close approximation of the texture of handblocked papers. There are over eighty patterns to choose from.

*Arthur Sanderson & Sons, Ltd.
Berners Street
London W1A 2JE, England

Exhaustive selection of decorative papers, including borders, embossed papers, chintzes, and many flocked papers.

*San Francisco Victoriana
2245 Palou Avenue
San Francisco, CA 94124
(415) 648-0313

Embossed wallcoverings and friezes, including anaglypta and supaglypta, along with a good selection of antique border papers.

Scalamandré Silks, Inc.
950 Third Avenue
New York, NY 10022
(212) 361-8800

Many historical papers, including the William Morris collection, which is carefully reproduced from nineteenth-century documents.

F. Schumacher & Company
939 Third Avenue
New York, NY 10022
(212) 644-5900

Many period prints, including French florals, damasks, and reproductions prepared in association with the Victorian Society of America.

*Shanker-Glendale Steel Corporation, Inc.
70-32 83rd Street
Glendale, NY 11385
(212) 326-1100

A fine selection of ceiling plates and metal cornice moldings.

*Stamford Wallpaper Company
153 Greenwich Avenue
Stamford, CT 06904
(203) 323-1123

A full line of reproduction papers is available.

Richard E. Thibaut
706 South 21st Street
Irvington, NJ 07111
(201) 399-7888

Adaptations of nineteenth-century designs and a good choice of flocked papers.

The Twigs
5700 Third Street
San Francisco, CA 94124
(415) 822-1626

Museum-quality papers, expertly documented and reproduced, including many that are suitable for Victorian interiors.

*The Wallpaper Works
749 Queen Street West
Toronto, Ontario M6J 1G1
Canada
(416) 366-1790

Original historic wallpapers dating back to the turn of the century.

Waterhouse Wallhangings
38 Wareham Street
Boston, MA 02118
(617) 423-7688

Original early-Victorian papers.

*Watts & Co., Ltd.
7 Tufton Street, Westminster
London SW1P 3QB
England

One of the venerable British ecclesiastical furnishings suppliers with a vast stock of mid- to late-1800's designs by such eminent artists as Augustin Pugin.

*Waverly Fabrics
58 West 40th Street
New York, NY 10018
(212) 644-5890

Attractive and moderately-priced small-figured patterns are available from this supplier of country-style papers and fabrics. The designs are appropriate for many early- to mid-Victorian interiors.

Zina Studios, Inc.
85 Purdy Avenue
Port Chester, NY 10573
(914) 937-5661

Superb documentary papers first executed for leading restoration projects and now available to the public.

Lighting

Alco Lightcraft Company
1424 West Alabama
Houston, TX 77006
(713) 526-0680

Custom-designed sconces and glass shades.

Art Directions
6120 Delmar
St. Louis, MO 63112
(314) 863-1895

Antique lighting devices of various types frequently in stock.

Brasslight, Inc.
90 Main Street
Nyack, NY 10960
(914) 353-0567

Quality brass reproductions of table and floor lamps.

Campbell Lamps
1108 Pottstown Pike
West Chester, PA 19380
(215) 696-8070

Wide selection of replacement glass shades.

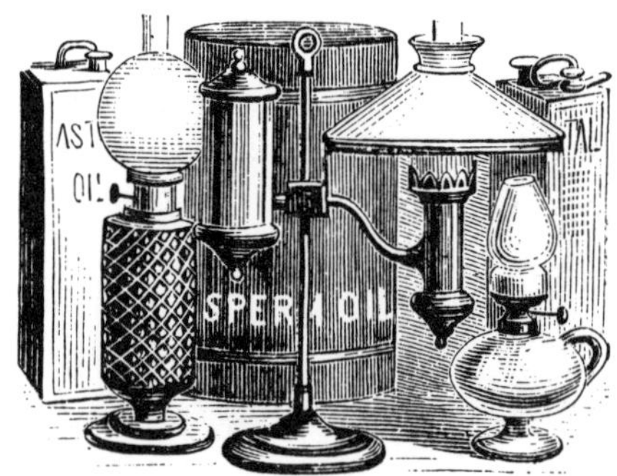

City Lights Antique Lighting
2226 Massachusetts Avenue
Cambridge, MA 02140
(617) 547-1490

Solid-brass floor lamps from the early electric period.

The Classic Illumination
431 Grove Street
Oakland, CA 94607
(415) 465-7786

A good source for fine, handcrafted reproduction lighting.

Crawford's Old House Store
301 McCall
Waukesha, WI 53186
(414) 542-0685

Replacement crystal prisms for chandeliers as well as other basic lighting supplies.

Custom House
Box 38, South Shore Drive
Owls Head, ME 04854
(207) 594-9281 or 236-4444

Victorian lampshades in various fabrics and lace.

Gargoyles, Ltd.
512 South Third Street
Philadelphia, PA 19147
(215) 629-1700

A good stock of antique fixtures from various American and European sources.

Greg's Antique Lighting
12005 Wilshire Boulevard
Los Angeles, CA 90025
(213) 478-5475

An excellent source of original Victorian lighting fixtures rewired for electricity.

Jo-El Shop
7120 Hawkins Creamery Road
Laytonsville, MD 20879
(301) 972-4100

A good selection of rare original glass shades, as well as the repair of fixtures and shades.

The Lamp Clinic
513 Morris Avenue
Summit, NJ 07901
(201) 273-1323

A good source for restored lamps and chandeliers as well as for repair work.

The London Venturers Company
2 Dock Square
Rockport, MA 01966
(617) 546-7161

Antique lighting restored and rewired.

Metropolitan Lighting Fixture Company, Inc.
1010 Third Avenue
New York, NY 10021
(212) 838-2425

Turn-of-the-century chandeliers with hanging crystals and burnished brass finish.

C. Neri Antiques & Interiors
313 South Street
Philadelphia, PA 19147
(215) 923-6669

One of the finest collections of antique nineteenth-century lighting fixtures.

Nowell's Inc.
490 Gate Five Road
Sausalito, CA 94965
(415) 332-4933

Reproduction lighting fixtures and museum-quality restoration of antique lighting devices.

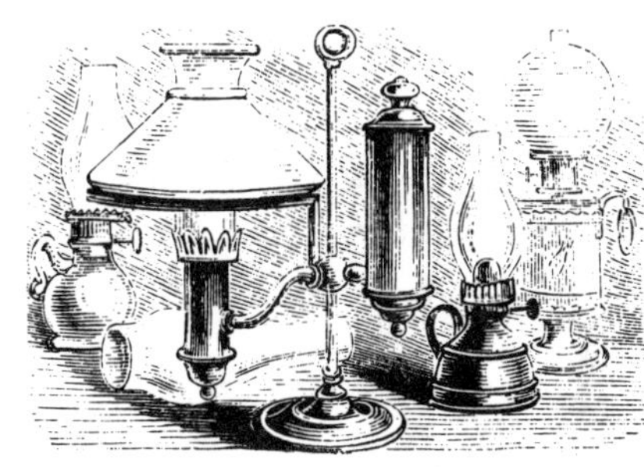

E. W. Pyfer
218 North Foley Avenue
Freeport, IL 61032
(815) 232-8968

Lamp repair and wiring services as well as a good stock of lamp parts.

Rejuvenation House Parts
4543 North Albina Avenue
Portland, OR 97217
(503) 282-3019

Solid-brass reproduction fixtures and a wide variety of shades.

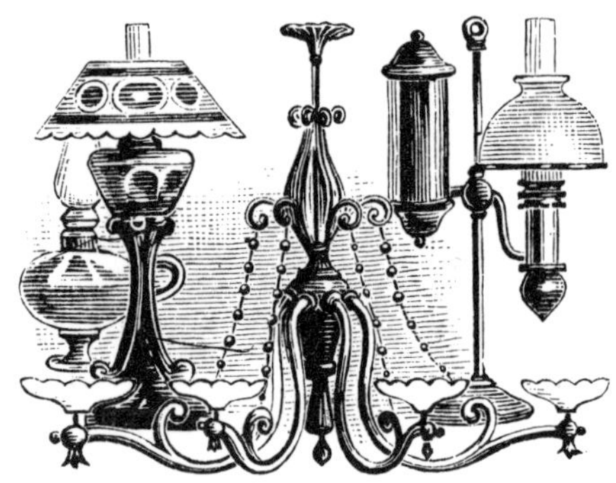

Roy Electric Company, Inc.
1054 Coney Island Avenue
Brooklyn, NY 11230
(212) 339-6311 or 761-7905

Reproduction and restored and rewired antique fixtures of style and craftsmanship.

St. Louis Antique Lighting Company
PO Box 8146
St. Louis, MO 63156
(314) 535-2770

Handsome period chandeliers.

Squaw Alley, Inc.
401 South Main Street
Naperville, IL 60540
(312) 357-0200

Well stocked with lamp converters, shades in fabric and glass, antique brass fixtures, and lamp parts.

Stanley Galleries Antiques
2118 North Clark Street
Chicago, IL 60614
(312) 281-1614

A good selection of antique chandeliers.

Valley Iron & Steel Company
29579 Awbrey Lane
Eugene, OR 97402
(503) 688-7741

Turn-of-the-century streetlight standards.

Victorian Lightcrafters Ltd.
PO Box 332
Slate Hill, NY 10973
(914) 355-1300

Solid-brass as well as less expensive reproduction lighting fixtures.

Victorian Reproduction Enterprises, Inc.
1601 Park Avenue S.
Minneapolis, MN 55404
(612) 338-3636

Reproduction fixtures, glass and cloth shades, Tiffany-style shades, and lighting parts.

Welsbach Lighting Inc.
240 Sargent Drive
New Haven, CT 06511
(203) 789-1710

An extensive line of Victorian outdoor lighting products from a pioneer in the field.

The Wrecking Bar of Atlanta
292 Moreland Avenue
Atlanta, GA 30307
(404) 525-0468

A continually changing supply of antique fixtures for many different purposes.

Yankee Craftsman
357 Commonwealth Road
Wayland, MA 01778
(617) 653-0031

Antique fixtures and custom designs as well as restoration and repairs by a master craftsman.

Decorative Painting

PAINT

Laura Ashley, Inc. (mail order)
Box 5308
Melville, NY 11747
(800) 523-6383

There are Ashley retail outlets across the United States; call the number above for the location of the shop nearest you.

Ashley is much better known for fabrics, but its vinyl matt emulsion and satin gloss paints present some interesting choices for period interiors.

Fuller-O'Brien Paints
PO Box 864
Brunswick, GA 31521
(912) 265-7650

The Heritage Cape May Color Collection includes colors appropriate for nineteenth-century interiors and exteriors.

Sherwin-Williams Company
PO Box 6939
Cleveland, OH 44101
(216) 566-2332

The Heritage Collection constitutes an excellent selection of authenticated colors for Victorian interiors and exteriors.

Wolf Paints
771 Ninth Avenue
New York, NY 10019
(212) 245-7777

An extensive line of materials for decorative painting, including brushes for stenciling, gilding, graining, marbling, stippling, and wood finishes. This company also carries an enormous range of paints and other types of finishes. Wolf will accept mail orders.

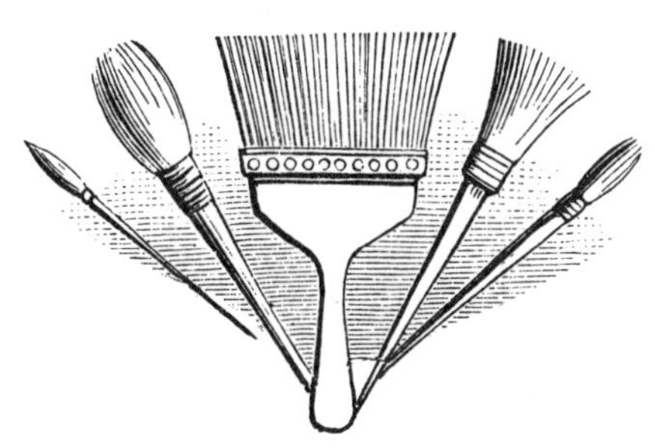

DECORATIVE PAINTERS

Larry Boyce
c/o George Zaffle
1073 Page Street
San Francisco, CA 94114
(415) 929-8410

Boyce can restore, adapt, or invent any type of decorative finish—including stenciling, marbling, and wood graining—to a client's specifications. He will also execute murals.

John Canning
132 Meeker Road
Southington, CT 06489
(203) 621-2188

An expert in researching and restoring all types of decorative paintings, including marbling, wood graining, and tortoiseshell finishes.

The Rambusch Company
40 West 13th Street
New York, NY 10011
(212) 675-0400

This talented multipurpose group can undertake large or small projects of considerable complexity.

Malcolm F. Robson
4308 Argonne Drive
Fairfax, VA 22032
(703) 978-5331

An English artist with many fine commissions to his credit, Robson is now working in the United States and will execute wood finishes and all types of decorative faux finishes.

Waterman-West
741 Ponce de Leon Court, Suite 4
Atlanta, GA 30308
(404) 874-9678

A group of craftsmen who will undertake all types of decorative finishes, including graining and marbling.

Roy Lewis Wingate
560 Green Street
San Francisco, CA 94133

An experienced artist in various faux decorative treatments and chinoiserie.

The Hearth

MANTELS

Art Directions
6120 Delmar
St. Louis, MO 63112
(314) 863-1895

Antique mantels are often included in the offerings of this architectural antiques outlet.

Gargoyles, Ltd.
512 South Third Street
Philadelphia, PA 19147
(215) 629-1700

A good source for antique mantels of wood, marble, and other materials.

William H. Jackson Company
3 East 47th Street
New York, NY 10017
(212) 752-9400

One of America's oldest suppliers of finely-crafted mantels and custom overmantels; tile mantel facings also available.

Chip LaPointe
186 Emerson Place
Brooklyn, NY 11205
(212) 857-8594

A master craftsman in wood who will undertake special commissions, including reproduction mantels.

Rosewood Ventures
Box 610, Port Maitland
Yarmouth County, Nova Scotia
Canada BOW 2V0
(902) 649-2782

Custom wood mantels are among the specialties of this reproduction firm.

Norman Vandal
PO Box 67
Roxbury, VT 05669
(802) 485-8380

A craftsman who can restore and recreate period mantelpieces in wood.

Wrecking Bar of Atlanta
292 Moreland Avenue, NE
Atlanta, GA 30307
(404) 525-0468

Antique mantels are a part of the regular stock of this supplier of architectural materials.

Ye Olde Mantel Shoppe
3800 N.E. Second Avenue
Miami, FL 33137
(305) 576-0225

Foreign and domestic antique and reproduction mantels in cast iron or pine.

THE PARLOR STOVE

Agape Antiques
Box 225
Saxtons River, VT 05154
(802) 869-2273

A wide range of restored stoves for the parlor.

Bow and Arrow Stoves
11 Hurley Street
Cambridge, MA 02138
(617) 492-1411

Importers of the famed circular Le Petit Godin, which warmed many Victorian parlors in Europe and North America.

Bryant Steel Works
RFD 2, Box 109
Thorndike, ME 04986
(207) 568-3663

A wide selection of antique parlor stoves, all restored to "like-new" condition.

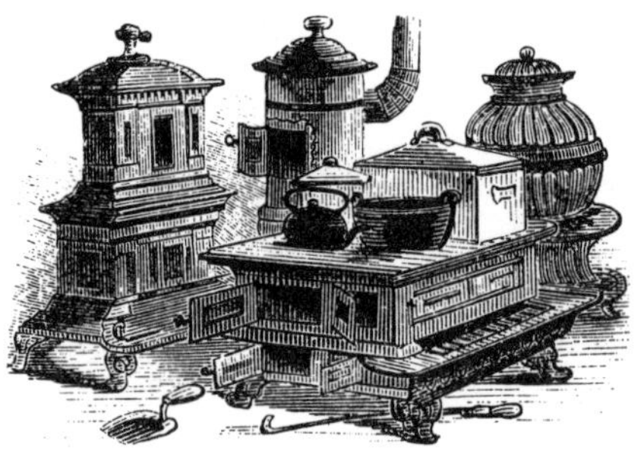

The Burning Log, Eastern Office
PO Box 438
Lebanon, NH 03766
(603) 448-4364

The Burning Log, Western Office
PO Box 8519
Aspen, CO 81611
(303) 925-8968

Suppliers of the ornate reproduction De Dietrich & Co. parlor stove.

Cumberland General Store
Route 3
Crossville, TN 38555
(615) 484-8481

A good selection of cast-iron stove grates and corrugated coal hods.

Lehman Hardware & Appliances
PO Box 41
Kidron, OH 44636
(216) 857-5441

An old-fashioned supplier of old-fashioned stoves and heating supplies still popular with the Amish of the Midwest.

Grampa's Wood Stoves
Box 492
Ware, MA 01082
(413) 967-6684

The sale, repair, and restoration of antique stoves for use with coal or wood.

THE KITCHEN HEARTH

Agape Antiques
Box 225
Saxtons River, VT 05154
(802) 869-2273

Restored cookstoves for coal and wood, made by major nineteenth-century firms.

Lehman Hardware & Appliances
Box 41
Kidron, OH 44636
(216) 857-5441

Traditional wood-burning kitchen stoves for the Amish are regularly supplied and resemble earlier models.

Pacific Lamp & Stove
PO Box 30610
Seattle, WA 98103
(800) 426-6721

A supplier of such famous wood/coal cookstoves as the Oval, restored and ready for use.

West Barnstable Stove Shop
Box 472
West Barnstable, MA 02668
(617) 362-9913

A good selection of Victorian cookstoves and stove parts; also undertakes restoration work.

DECORATIVE TILES FOR THE HEARTH AND MANTEL

Architectural Terra Cotta & Tile Ltd.
727 South Dearborn, Suite 1012
Chicago, IL 60605
(312) 786-0229

Experts at restoring and recreating period tilework for use throughout the house.

Laura Ashley, Inc. (mail order)
Box 5308
Melville, NY 11747
(800) 523-6383

There are Ashley retail outlets across the United States; contact the number above for the location of the shop nearest you.

Attractive ceramic tiles in nineteenth-century floral and geometric designs.

Berkshire Porcelain Studios
Deerfield Avenue
Shelburne Falls, MA 01370
(413) 625-9447

Custom-made ceramic tiles for any period.

Country Floors
300 East 61st Street
New York, NY 10021
(212) 758-7414

This retail and mail-order firm offers an extensive list of foreign and domestic decorative tiles.

William H. Jackson Company
3 East 47th Street
New York, NY 10017
(212) 753-9400

A wide selection of reproduction tiles as well as a supply of antique tiles.

Helen Williams
12643 Hortense Street
North Hollywood, CA 91604
(213) 761-2756

Although primarily a dealer in early Dutch Delft tiles, Helen Williams can assist in the search for Victorian period pieces.

Fabrics

Documentary designs and adaptations of historical patterns suitable for Victorian interiors are produced and/or distributed by a number of American, Canadian, and English firms. Distribution of fabrics and carpets to individual buyers is often limited to interior designers or design departments of major retail outlets. The firms marked with an asterisk are those which sell directly to the public either through retail outlets or by mail order. All the firms listed will provide information on the type and availability of their offerings. The reader may find that some of the best reproduction fabrics may be found from time to time in fabric centers and surplus shops as it is the practice of manufacturers to occasionally discount lines and offer them to the general public.

*Laura Ashley, Inc. (mail order)
Box 5308
Melville, NY 11747
(800) 523-6383

There are Ashley retail outlets across the United States; contact the number above for the location of the shop nearest you.

The fanciful floral and small-figure printed cottons available from Ashley span the nineteenth century and are most appropriate for informal and country interiors.

*Amazon Vinegar & Pickling Works Drygoods
2218 East 11th Street
Davenport, IA 52803
(309) 786-3504

An amazing selection of damasks and satins as well as Osnaburg , a coarse cotton.

Brunschwig & Fils, Inc.
979 Third Avenue
New York, NY 10022
(212) 838-7878

Expert reproductions of Victorian fabrics of American, English, and French origin, many in documentary colors. The English glazed chintzes and woven upholstery textiles—including horsehair and plush—are especially fine. Brunschwig also undertakes embossing from nineteenth-century rollers.

Clarence House
40 East 57th Street
New York, NY 10022
(212) 752-2890

This supplier is well known for its elegant English printed cottons.

Cyrus Clark Company
267 Fifth Avenue
New York, NY 10016
(212) 684-5312

Good adaptations of traditional chintz designs at reasonable prices.

Cowtan & Tout
979 Third Avenue
New York, NY 10022
(212) 753-4488

Silkscreened and handblocked prints as well as a large selection of documentary English chintzes.

Rose Cummings Chintzes
232 East 59th Street
New York, NY 10022
(212) 758-0844

As the name indicates, this firm specializes in cotton chintzes, most of them glazed and of English origin.

Decorators Walk
171 East 56th Street
New York, NY 10022
(212) 355-5300

Linen damasks based on various Victorian revival patterns, several types of synthetic batiste and lace, and 100% cotton dotted Swiss and Swiss lawn are available through this supplier.

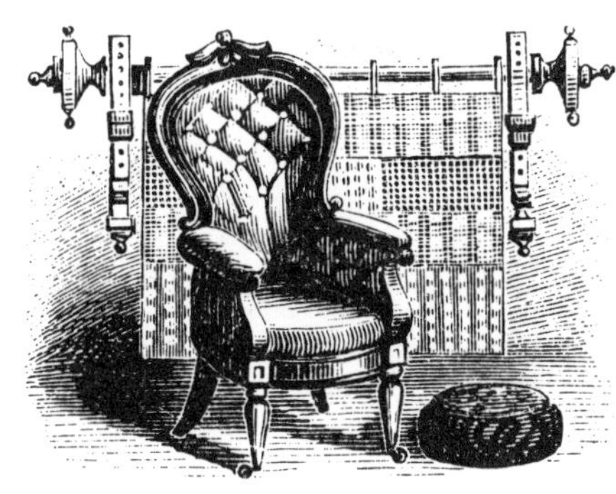

Fonthill
979 Third Avenue
New York, NY 10022
(212) 751-8666

A source for 100% cotton glazed chintzes.

Greef
155 East 56th Street
New York, NY 10022
(212) 288-5060

A variety of lightweight cottons and glazed chintzes is reproduced as part of museum collections. Greef is also a good source for 100% cotton lace and for Tambour curtaining.

Hamilton-Adams
104 West 49th Street
New York, NY 10018
(212) 221-0800

An importer of many types of linen weaves.

S. M. Hexter
2800 Superior Avenue
Cleveland, OH 44114
(216) 696-0146

Among period designs, many of them excellent adaptations, is a handsome collection of paisley prints in 100% cotton.

*Peter Jones
Sloane Square
London SW1, England

A leading English supplier of expertly made lace, including 100% cotton curtaining. This firm also carries pure white cotton muslin and plain, unpatterned, coarsely-woven linens. Jones also offers an interesting selection of Italian furnishing materials, including silky stripes and sprigged florals in Victorian revival designs.

Lee-Jofa
979 Third Avenue
New York, NY 10022
(212) 889-3900

A broad selection of English printed cottons, many based on documentary sources, and voile, wool rep, mohair velour, and horsehair weaves.

*Lovelia Enterprises, Inc.
356 East 41st Street
New York, NY 10017

A supplier of tapestries for hanging or draping, as well as tapestry weaves for chair tops and seat covers.

Scalamandré Silks, Inc.
950 Third Avenue
New York, NY 10022
(212) 361-8800

Scalamandré is one of the few American fabric houses to manufacture period textiles domestically, including some of the finest materials used in such places as the White House and many state executive mansions. The firm is also a major importer of a wide variety of special weaves and printed fabrics. A large selection of documentary patterns is available in lightweight cottons as well as upholstery-weight silks, wools, and blends of natural and synthetic materials.

F. Schumacher & Company
939 Third Avenue
New York, NY 10022
(212) 644-5900

A pioneer in documentary period fabrics, Schumacher introduced the important and useful Victorian

Collection. A full range of lightweight prints and upholstery-weight fabrics, produced domestically and imported, is available.

Stroheim and Romann
155 East 56th Street
New York, NY 10022
(212) 691-0700

In addition to several cotton chintzes in documentary designs, this firm offers authenticated reproductions from the Winterthur Museum collection, including leathers. Some of the Winterthur materials might be used appropriately in early-Victorian settings.

*Sunflower Studio
2851 Road B½
Grand Junction, CO 81501
(303) 242-3883

Master weaver Constance La Lena produces some of the most difficult-to-find Colonial and Victorian reproduction fabrics. You can depend on her for hand-woven wool baize, linen, linen and cotton fustian, Osnaburg, and upholstery serge.

The Twigs
5700 Third Street
San Francisco, CA 94124
(415) 822-1626

A select and expertly-manufactured collection of hand-screened fabrics in nineteenth-century designs.

Ulster Weaving Company
148 Madison Avenue
New York, NY 10018
(212) 684-5534

A supplier of linen weaves.

Waverly Fabrics
58 West 40th Street
New York, NY 10018
(212) 644-5890

Reasonably-priced cotton prints and damasks based on English and American Victorian designs, many of which can be found in fabric shops coast-to-coast.

RUGS AND CARPETS

*Colefax & Fowler Designs Ltd.
39 Brook Street
London W1Y 1AU, England
(01) 439-2231

Brussels and Wilton-weave carpets in absolutely perfect nineteenth-century English designs.

*Good Stenciling
Box 387
Dublin, NH 03444
(603) 563-8021

You can depend on Nancy Good

Cayford to produce designs which are appropriate for Victorian floorcloths. There are stock patterns available to choose from, but custom work is also undertaken.

*Langhorne Carpet Company
PO Box 175
Penndel, PA 19047
(215) 757-5155

Custom-made Wilton carpets in Victorian-period designs.

*Patterson, Flynn and Martin
950 Third Avenue
New York, NY 10022
(212) 751-6414

Among many stock offerings are some delightful traditional patterns that would complement many period interiors.

Scalamandré Silks, Inc.
950 Third Avenue
New York, NY 10022
(212) 361-8800

A major supplier, manufacturer, and importer of authentic carpeting. Brussels, Wilton, and Axminster designs are available. Most work is custom-ordered.

F. Schumacher & Company
939 Third Avenue
New York, NY 10022
(212) 644-5900

A major supplier of carpeting for period interiors, as well as a source for adaptations.

Stark Carpets
979 Third Avenue
New York, NY 10022
(212) 752-9000

A dependable source of traditional designs as well as reproduction Wiltons commissioned for restorations.

*Sunflower Studio
2851 Road B½
Grand Junction, CO 81501
(303) 242-3883

An excellent source for striped Venetian carpeting suitable for runners in hallways and bedrooms.

ACKNOWLEDGMENTS

The authors gratefully acknowledge the valuable assistance of S. Allen Chambers, Jr., and Denys Peter Myers of the Historic American Buildings Survey, National Park Service, Department of the Interior, Washington, D.C.; Mary Ison of the Prints and Photographs Division, Library of Congress, Washington, D.C.; William Seale, Alexandria, Va.; and James Roper, Little Rock, Ark., in locating and documenting many of the illustrations included in this book. Special thanks are also owed to Muriel Palmer, executive director of The Park-McCullough House, North Bennington, Vt.; John Ashbery, David Kermani, and many private homeowners who graciously permitted photography of their houses.

The photographers represented in *American Victorian* contributed significantly to the presentation of the richness and spirit of Victorian architecture and decoration. We wish to thank especially Eric Borg, Middlebury, Vt.; Mark Gottlieb, Palo Alto, Ca.; Michael Kanouff, Mill Valley, Ca.; Van Jones Martin, Savannah, Ga.; Chad Slattery, Los Angeles, Ca.; Walter Smalling, Washington, D.C.; and Jack E. Boucher and the other photographers of the Historic American Buildings Survey.

ILLUSTRATION CREDITS

In this list of photographic credits, the abbreviation HABS stands for the Historic American Buildings Survey. A name within parentheses after HABS indicates the name of a HABS photographer. Other abbreviations include: a (above), b (below), c (center), l (left), ll (lower left), lr (lower right), r (right), rb (right bottom, rc (right center), rt (right top), ul (upper left), and ur (upper right).

Frontispiece: photograph by Michael Kanouff.

Chapter 1: p. 10, courtesy of the Wrecking Bar of Atlanta; pp. 12-13, HABS (Jack E. Boucher); pp. 14-15, HABS; p. 16, photographs by Mark Gottlieb (ll, lr), HABS (ul); p. 17, HABS (ul), The Main Street Press (lr); p. 18, The Library of Congress (ul), HABS (Jack E. Boucher) (ll), HABS (lr); p. 19, HABS (ur, lr), photograph by Michael Kanouff (ur); p. 20, HABS (Jack E. Boucher); p. 21, HABS (ll), HABS (Thom Loughman) (ur), photograph by Mark Gottlieb (lr).

Chapter 2: p. 22, HABS (Jack E. Boucher); p. 24, photograph by Michael Kanouff; p. 25, photograph by Michael Kanouff (l), photograph by Eric Borg (r); p. 26, HABS (Jack E. Boucher); p. 27, HABS (ul, ll), The Main Street Press (r); p. 28, HABS (Jack E. Boucher); p. 29, photographs by Michael Kanouff; p. 30, courtesy of Sandra Brauer/Stained Glass (ll), HABS (Jack E. Boucher) (ur, lr); p. 31, HABS (George Eisenman) (l), courtesy of Walton Stained Glass (ur), courtesy of Architectural Emphasis, Inc. (lr); p. 32, photograph by Michael Kanouff (a), photograph by Eric Borg (b); pp. 33-34, HABS (Jack E. Boucher); p. 35, ibid. (l), HABS (Stanley Schwartz) (r); p. 36, The Main Street Press (ul), courtesy of Pocahontas Hdwe. & Glass (ll), HABS (Jack E. Boucher) (r); p. 37, photograph by Chad Slattery; p. 38, photograph by Michael Kanouff; p. 39, HABS (ll), HABS (Jack E. Boucher) (ur); The Main Street Press (lr); p. 40, photograph by Eric Borg; p. 41, HABS (Jack E. Boucher) (ul), The Main Street Press (ur), HABS (Kenn Knackstedt) (ll, lr); p. 42, HABS (Jack E. Boucher) (l), courtesy of Gargoyles Ltd. (lr); p. 43, courtesy of Cumberland Woodcraft (ul), HABS (Jack E. Boucher) (ll), courtesy of Gargoyles Ltd. (r); p. 44, The Main Street Press; p. 45, HABS (Jack E. Boucher) (ur, lr), HABS (ll), The Main Street Press (ur); p. 46, ibid. (ll), courtesy of San Francisco Victoriana (ur), HABS (Jack E. Boucher) (lr); p. 47, ibid. (ul, ll), The Main Street Press (ur); pp. 48-49, HABS (Jack E. Boucher).

Chapter 3: p. 50, HABS (Jack E. Boucher); pp. 52-53, The Main Street Press; p. 54, HABS (Jack E. Boucher) (ll), The Main Street Press and Horton Brasses (remainder); p. 55, HABS (Jack E. Boucher) (ll, lr), The Main Street Press (ur); p. 56, HABS; p. 57, ibid. (ul), The Main Street Press (ll).

Chapter 4: p. 58, The Main Street Press; p. 60, photograph by Walter Smalling; p. 61, courtesy of Scalamandré, Inc.; p.

62, ibid. (a), HABS (b); p. 63, The Main Street Press; p. 64, courtesy of Scalamandré, Inc.; p. 65, The Library of Congress; p. 66, HABS; p. 67, The Main Street Press; p. 68, courtesy of Scalamandré, Inc.; p. 69, photograph by Chad Slattery; p. 70, photograph by Michael Kanouff; p. 71, photograph by Walter Smalling; p. 72, photograph by Eric Borg; p. 73, *clockwise from ur:* HABS (Jack E. Boucher), courtesy of San Francisco Victoriana, courtesy of Chelsea Decorative Metal, HABS.

Chapter 5: p. 74, photograph by Van Jones Martin; p. 76, photograph by Michael Kanouff; p. 77, courtesy of Greg's Antique Lighting (l, r), The Main Street Press (c); p. 78, HABS (a), The Main Street Press (b); p. 79, courtesy of Greg's Antique Lighting; p. 80, HABS (Jack E. Boucher); p. 81, ibid. (l), courtesy of Greg's Antique Lighting (r); p. 82, HABS (a), The Main Street Press; p. 83, *clockwise from ul:* HABS (Jack E. Boucher), ibid., courtesy of The London Venturers Company, ibid., ibid., The Main Street Press; p. 84, HABS; p. 85, courtesy of Greg's Antique Lighting (second from l), The Main Street Press (remainder); p. 86, HABS (Jack E. Boucher) (ul), The Main Street Press (ur), courtesy of Yankee Craftsman (ll), The Main Street Press (lr); p. 87, HABS (Robert Thall) (ul), The Main Street Press (ur, ul, lr); p. 88, HABS (Jack E. Boucher); p. 89, *top row:* courtesy of Victorian Lightcrafters, *center row:* courtesy of Campbell Lamps, *bottom row:* courtesy of Greg's Antique Lighting (l), courtesy of Campbell Lamps (c, r); p. 90, courtesy of Greg's Antique Lighting (ul, ll), The Library of Congress (c), The Main Street Press (r); p. 91, HABS (Jack E. Boucher) (ul), courtesy of The London Venturers Company (ur), The Library of Congress (ll), HABS (Jack E. Boucher); p. 92, ibid.; p. 93, ibid. (ul), The Main Street Press (remainder).

Chapter 6: p. 94, photograph by Chad Slattery; p. 95, HABS (Jack E. Boucher) (l), courtesy of Scalamandré, Inc. (r); p. 97, HABS (Laurence E. Tilley) (a), courtesy of Scalamandré, Inc. (b); pp. 98-99, HABS; p. 100, photograph by Michael Kanouff (a), HABS (Robert Thall) (b); p. 101, HABS (a), HABS (Jack E. Boucher) (b); pp.102-105, photographs by Chad Slattery; p. 106, The Main Street Press; p. 107, HABS (Jack E. Boucher) (l), courtesy of Marguerite Deats Raesly (r).

Chapter 7: p. 108, photograph by Van Jones Martin; p. 110, photograph by Eric Borg; p. 111, photograph by Michael Kanouff; pp. 112-17, The Main Street Press; p. 118, HABS (Cervin Robinson) (a), HABS (Robert Thall) (b); p. 119, The Library of Congress; p. 120, HABS; p. 121, ibid. (ul, ur), HABS (Hans Padelt) (ll), HABS (Robert Thall) (lr); p. 122, HABS (Jack E. Boucher); p. 123, The Library of Congress (ul), HABS (Jack E. Boucher) (ll), HABS (ur); p. 124, ibid.; p. 125, HABS (Jack E. Boucher) (l), The Main Street Press (r); pp. 126-27, HABS (Jack E. Boucher); p. 128, HABS (a), HABS (Jack E. Boucher) (b); p. 129, photograph by Eric Borg (a), HABS (b); p. 130, The Library of Congress; p. 131, courtesy of Scalamandré, Inc.; p. 132, photograph by Eric Borg (a), photograph by Michael Kanouff (b); p. 133, HABS (a), The Library of Congress (b); p. 134, The Main Street Press (ll), HABS (rt, rc, rb); p. 135, ibid. (a), The Main Street Press (r); p. 136, HABS (Jack E. Boucher); p. 137, ibid. (a), The Library of Congress (b).

Chapter 8: p. 138, HABS (Jack E. Boucher); p. 140, HABS (ur), HABS (Jack E. Boucher) (lr); p. 141, *clockwise from ul:* HABS, HABS (Jack E. Boucher), ibid., HABS, HABS (Cervin Robinson), HABS; p. 142, The Main Street Press; p. 143, HABS (Jack E. Boucher) (ul, ur), HABS (George A. Eisenman (ll), courtesy of Grampa's Wood Stoves (lr); p. 144, HABS (Jack E. Boucher) (l), The Main Street Press (lr); p. 145, ibid. (ul), HABS (Jack E. Boucher) (ll, lr); p. 146, The Library of Congress (ur), HABS (Cervin Robinson) (r); p. 147, The Main Street Press; p. 148, New Jersey State Museum (ll), HABS (Jack E. Boucher) (r); p. 148, The Smithsonian Institution (ul, ur, lr), The Main Street Press (ll).

Chapter 9: p. 150, The Main Street Press; p. 151, HABS (Hans Padelt) (ul, ll), The Main Street Press (lr); p. 153, The Library of Congress; p. 154, photograph by Eric Borg; p. 155, courtesy of Scalamandré, Inc.; p. 156, courtesy of Focal Point, Inc. (l), The Library of Congress (r); p. 157, photograph by Walter Smalling; p. 158, HABS (l), courtesy of Scalamandré, Inc. (r); p. 159, photograph by Eric Borg; p. 160, HABS (ur), The Library of Congress (b); p. 161, courtesy of Scalamandré, Inc. (ul), The Main Street Press (ur), courtesy of Peter Jones (ll, lr); p. 162, photograph by

Eric Borg; p. 163, *clockwise from ul:* courtesy of Scalamandré, Inc., ibid., The Main Street Press, courtesy of Langhorne Carpet Co.; p. 164, photograph by Walter Smalling; p. 165, The Library of Congress; p. 166, courtesy of Scalamandré, Inc. (ll, ur), courtesy of Schumacher; p. 167, The Main Street Press; p. 168, courtesy of Brunschwig & Fils (l), courtesy of Scalamandré, Inc. (r); p. 169, courtesy of Brunschwig & Fils (ul), courtesy of Schumacher (ur), courtesy of Scalamandré, Inc. (lr).

Chapter 10: p. 170, photograph by Walter Smalling; p. 172, The Main Street Press (ll), New Jersey State Museum (ur), courtesy of Scalamandré, Inc. (lr); p. 173, *clockwise from ul:* The Main Street Press, The Library of Congress, collection of Martin Greif, courtesy of Marguerite Deats Raesly, ibid., ibid., The Main Street Press, ibid.; pp. 174-77, ibid.; pp. 178-79, collection of Jean Bach; p. 180, The New-York Historical Society (uc), private collection (lr); p. 181, Smithsonian Institution (ul), The Main Street Press (ll), HABS (Jack E. Boucher) (r); p. 182, The Main Street Press; p. 183, New Jersey State Museum (l), Smithsonian Institution (rt), The Main Street Press and The Smithsonian Institution (rc), The Smithsonian Institution (rb); p. 184, HABS (Jack E. Boucher) (ur), The Main Street Press (ll), courtesy of The Lyndhurst Corporation (lr); p. 185, *clockwise from ul:* courtesy of The Lyndhurst Corporation, ibid., The Newark Museum, The Main Street Press, ibid., ibid., M. H. de Young Memorial Museum; p. 186, The Main Street Press; p. 187, *clockwise from ul:* New Jersey State Museum, Philadelphia Museum of Art, The Main Street Press, New Jersey State Museum, The Brooklyn Museum; pp. 188-90, The Main Street Press; p. 191, The Main Street Press (photograph by George J. Fistrovich); p. 192, photograph by Walter Smalling.

BIBLIOGRAPHY

Ames, Kenneth L. "Grand Rapids Furniture at the Time of the Centennial." *Winterthur Portfolio* 10 (1975).

______. "What is the Neo-Grec?" *Nineteenth Century* 2, no. 2 (Summer 1976): 12-21.

Ames, Winslow. "Inside Victorian Walls." *Victorian Studies* 5, no. 2 (1961): 151-62.

Ayres, William S. *The Main Street Pocket Guide to Toys.* Pittstown, N.J.: Main Street, 1984.

Bach, Jean. *The Main Street Pocket Guide to Dolls.* Pittstown, N.J.: Main Street, 1983.

Beecher, Catherine and Harriet Beecher Stowe. *The American Woman's Home.* 1869. Reprint. Hartford, Conn.: Stowe-Day Foundation, 1975.

Bishop, Adele and Cile Lord. *The Art of Decorative Stenciling.* New York: Penguin, 1978.

Blackall, Clarence Howard. *Builders' Hardware: A Manual for Architects, Builders, and House Finishers.* Boston, 1890.

Bridgman, Harriet and Elizabeth Drury, eds. *The Encyclopedia of Victoriana.* New York: Macmillan, 1975.

Burke, James H. *The Main Street Pocket Guide to Sterling and Silver Plate.* Pittstown, N.J.: Main Street, 1984.

Butler, Joseph T. *American Furniture from the First Colonies to World War I.* London: Tribune Books, 1973.

______. *American Antiques, 1800-1900.* New York, 1965.

Caulfield, Sophia and Blanche C. Saward. *Encyclopedia of Victorian Needlework.* 2 vols. 1882. Reprint. New York: Dover, 1972.

Church, Ella Rodman. *How to Furnish a Home.* New York, 1883.

Clark, Fiona. *William Morris: Wallpapers and Chintzes.* London: Academy, 1973.

Clark, Kenneth. *The Gothic Revival.* London: Murray, 1962.

Cleveland, Rose E., ed. *Social Mirror: A Complete Treatise on the Laws, Rules, and Usages that Govern Our Most Refined Homes and Social Circles.* St. Louis, 1888.

Clifford, Chandler Robbins. *Period Decoration.* New York, 1901.

Cook, Clarence. *The House Beautiful: Essays on Beds, Tables, Stools, and Candlesticks.* 1878. Reprint. Croton-on-Hudson, N.Y.: North River, 1980.

______. *What Shall We Do With Our Walls?* New York, 1880.

Cooke, Lawrence S. *Lighting in America.* Rev. ed. Pittstown, N.J.: Main Street, 1984.

Cooper, Nicholas. *The Opulent Eye: Late Victorian and Edwardian Taste in Interior Design.* London: Architectural Press, 1976.

Davidson, Marshall B., ed. *American Heritage: Three Centuries of American Antiques..* New York: Bonanza Books, 1979.

Denker, Ellen and Bert. *The Warner Collector's Guide to North American Pottery and Porcelain.* New York: Warner Books, 1982.

Dittrick, Mark and Diane Kender Dittrick. *Decorative Hardware.* New York: Hearst Books, 1982.

Downing, Andrew J. *The Architecture of Country Houses, with Remarks on Interiors, Furniture.* 1850. Reprint. New York: Dover, 1969.

______. *Cottage Residences.* 1873. Reprint. New York: Dover, 1981.

Eastlake, Charles L. *Hints on Household Taste.* 4th ed. 1878. Reprint. New York: Dover, 1969.

Fairclough, Oliver and Emmeline Learly. *Textiles by William Morris and Morris and Company 1861-1940.* London: Thames and Hudson, 1981.

Foley, Martha Mix. *The American House.* New York: Harper & Row, 1980.

Frangiamore, Catherine Lynn. *Wallpapers in Historic Preservation.* Washington, D.C.: National Park Service, U.S. Department of the Interior, 1977.

Freeman, John. *Furniture for the Victorian House from the Works of Andrew Jackson Downing and J. C. Doudon.* Watkins Glen, N.Y.: American Life Foundation, 1968.

______. *Wallace Nutting's Colonial Revival.* Watkins Glen, N.Y.: American Life Foundation, 1969.

French, Lillie H. *Homes and Their Decoration.* New York, 1903.

Garrett, Elisabeth Donaghy, ed. *The Antiques Book of Victorian Interiors.* New York: Crown Publishers, 1981.

Gowans, Alan. *Images of American Living: Four Centuries of Architecture and Furniture as Cultural Expression.* Philadelphia: Lippincott, 1964.

Grant, Ian, ed. *Great Interiors.* New York, 1967.

Greysmith, Brenda. *Wallpaper.* New York: Macmillan, 1976.

Grow, Lawrence. *Classic Old House Plans.* Pittstown, N.J.: Main Street, 1984.

______. *The Fourth Old House Catalogue.* Pittstown, N.J.: Main Street, 1984.

______. *The Old House Book of Bedrooms.* New York: Warner Books, 1980.

______. *The Old House Book of Kitchens and Dining Rooms.* New York: Warner Books, 1981.

______. *The Old House Book of Living Rooms and Parlors.* New York: Warner Books, 1980.

______. *The Old House Book of Outdoor Living Spaces.* New York: Warner Books, 1981.

______. *The Warner Collector's Guide to Pressed Glass.* New York: Warner Books, 1982.

Handlin, David P. *The American Home, Architecture and Society, 1815-1915.* Boston: Little, Brown, 1979.

Hanks, David, ed. *Victorian, Gothic, and Renaissance Revival Furniture.* Philadelphia, 1972.

Innes, Jocasta. *Magic Paint: The Complete Guide to Decorative Finishes.* New York: Van Nostrand Reinhold, 1981.

Jones, Mrs. C. S. *Household Elegancies: Suggestions in Household Art and Tasteful Home Decoration.* New York, 1875.

Labine, Clem, ed.*The Old-House Journal Compendium.* New York: Overlook, 1980.

Lancaster, Clay. *New York Interiors at the Turn of the Century.* New York: Dover, 1977.

Leslie, Miss [Eliza]. *A Manual of Domestic Economy for Town and Country.* 7th ed. Philadelphia, 1844.

Lichten, Frances. *The Decorative Art of Victoria's Era.* New York: Scribner's, 1951.

Loth, Calder and Julius Sadler Trousdale, Jr. *The Only Proper Style: Gothic Architecture in America.* Boston: New York Graphic Society, 1975.

Lynes, Russell. *The Tastemakers.* 1954. Reprint. New York: Dover, 1980.

Lynn, Catherine. *Wallpaper in America from the Seventeenth Century to World War I.* New York: Norton, 1980.

Maass, John. *The Gingerbread Age: A View of Victorian America.* New York: Greenwich House, 1983.

______. *The Victorian Home in America.* New York: Hawthorne, 1972.

Mackson, I. *American Architecture, Interiors, and Furniture During the Latter Part of the 19th Century.* Boston, 1900.

Madigan, Mary Jean. "The Influence of Charles Locke Eastlake on American Furniture Manufacture, 1870-1890." *Winterthur Portfolio* 10 (1975).

Mayhew, Edgar and Minor Myers, Jr. *A Documentary History of American Interiors.* New York: Scribner's, 1980.

The Metropolitan Museum of Art. *19th-Century America: Furniture and Other Decorative Arts.* Greenwich, Conn.: New York Graphic Society, 1970.

Morland, Frank A. *Practical Decorative Upholstery.* 1890. Reprint, edited by Martha Gandy Fales. New York: Dutton, 1979.

Moss, Rodger W. *Century of Color: Exterior Decoration for American Buildings, 1820-1920.* Watkins Glen, N.Y.: American Life Foundation, 1981.

Mumford, Lewis. *The Brown Decades: A Study of the Arts in America, 1865-1895.* 1931. Reprint. New York: Dover, 1971.

Myers, Denys Peter. *American Gas Lighting.* Washington, 1978.

Nylander, Jane C. *Fabrics for Historic Buildings.* Washington, D.C.: Preservation Press, 1983.

Nylander, Richard C. *Wallpapers for Historic Buildings.* Washington, D.C.: Preservation Press, 1983.

Old-House Journal, The. Brooklyn, N.Y.: The Old-House Journal Corp., 1973—.

Otto, Celia Jackson. *American Furniture of the 19th Century.* New York, 1965.

Page, Marian. *Historic Houses Restored and Preserved.* New York: Whitney Library of Design, 1976.

Parry, Linda. *William Morris Textiles.* New York: Viking, 1983.

Peterson, Harold L. *American Interiors from Colonial Times to the Late Victorians.* New York: Scribner's, 1979.

Poppeliers, John C., S. Allen Chambers, Jr., and Nancy B. Schwartz. *What Style Is It? A Guide to American Architecture.* Washington, D.C.: Preservation Press, 1983.

Praz, Mario. *An Illustrated History of Interior Decorating from Pompeii to Art Nouveau.* New York: Thames and Hudson, 1982.

Sanford, Bigelow Carpet Company. *A Century of Carpet- and Rug-Making in America.* New York, 1925.

Schaefer, Herwin. *Nineteenth Century Modern: The Functional Tradition in Victorian Design.* New York: Praeger, 1970.

Schorsch, Anita. *The Main Street Pocket Guide to American Clocks.* Pittstown, N.J.: Main Street, 1983.

Seale, William. *Recreating the Historic House Interior.* Nashville, Tenn.: American Association for State and Local History, 1979.

______. *The Tasteful Interlude: American Interiors Through the Camera's Eye, 1860-1917.* Reprint. Nashville, Tenn.: American Association for State and Local History, 1980.

Teynac, Françoise, Pierre Nolot, and Jean-Denis Vivian. *Wallpaper: A History.* New York: Rizzoli, 1982.

Varney, Almon C. *Our Homes and Their Ornaments.* Detroit, 1881.

Vaux, Calvert. *Villas and Cottages.* 2nd ed. 1864. Reprint. New York: Dover, 1970.

von Zweck, Dina, ed. *The Woman's Day Dictionary of Furniture.* Secaucus, N.J.: Citadel, 1983.

______. *The Woman's Day Dictionary of Glass.* Secaucus, N.J.: Citadel, 1983.

Weymiss, Robert and B. B. Whineray. *Victorian Furniture.* London, 1962.

Wharton, Edith and Ogden Codman, Jr. *The Decoration of Houses.* 1897. Reprint. New York: Norton, 1978.

Wheeler, Candace. *Principles of Home Decoration.* New York, 1908.

Whiffen, Marcus. *American Architecture Since 1780.* Cambridge: M.I.T. Press, 1969.

Woodward, George E. *Woodward's Architecture and Rural Art.* Nos. I and II. 1867-68. Reprint. Watkins Glen, N.Y.: American Life Foundation, 1978.

INDEX